INTERNATIONAL TAX TREATMENT

OF

COMMON LAW TRUSTS

40th Congress IFA
New York 1986

INTERNATIONAL TAX TREATMENT
of
COMMON LAW TRUSTS

INTERNATIONAL FISCAL ASSOCIATION

Proceedings of a Seminar held in New York
in 1986 during the 40th Congress of the
International Fiscal Association

Vol. 11b

KLUWER LAW AND TAXATION PUBLISHERS
DEVENTER – ANTWERP

LONDON – FRANKFURT – BOSTON – NEW YORK

Distribution in the USA and *Canada:*
Kluwer Law and Taxation Publishers
101 Philip Drive
Norwell, Massachusetts 02061
USA

Library of Congress Cataloging-in-Publication Data

International tax treatment of common law trusts.

(IFA Congress seminar series; 11b)
1. Trusts and trustees–Taxation–Congresses.
I. International Fiscal Association. Congress (40th : 1986 : New York, N.Y.) II. Series.
K4536.T78A55 1986 341.7'5 87–26149

D/1988/2664/17

ISBN 90–6544–346–0

INTERNATIONAL TAX TREATMENT OF COMMON LAW TRUSTS

Proceedings of a Seminar held in New York in 1986 during the 40th Congress of the International Fiscal Association*

Chairman of the Seminar
Professor H. Dale (United States)
Professor of Law, New York University; Counsel, Cadwalader, Wickersham & Taft, New York

Secretary of the Seminar
Mr. Joseph de Carlo (United States)
Cadwalader, Wickersham & Taft, New York

Panelists
P. Gillioz (Switzerland)
Tavernier, Gillioz, de Preux Dorsaz, Geneva

J. Killius (Germany)
Strobl, Killius & Vorbrugg, Munich

J. King (Australia)
Mallesons Stephen Jacques, New York

Professor D. Trautman (United States)
Professor of Law, Harvard University

F. Tripet (France)
International Tax Consultant, Paris

* *The views expressed are those of the authors and not necessarily those of the International Fiscal Association*

IFA CONGRESS SEMINAR SERIES*

1. Work in Intergovernmental Organizations on Transnational Companies (Congress 1976)
2. The Revised OECD Model Double Taxation Convention on Income and Capital (Congress 1977)
3. Fiscal Policy and Tax Structures in the Pacific Region (Congress 1978)
4. UN Draft Model Taxation Convention (Congress 1979)
5. Recourse to Tax Havens – Use and Abuse (Congress 1980)
6. Taxation of the Income Arising from the International Seabed (Congress 1981)
7. Imputation Systems – Objectives and Consequences (Congress 1982)
8. Tax Policy towards the National Heritage (Congress 1983)
9. Adjustments for Tax Purposes in Highly Inflationary Economies (Congress 1984)
10. International Tax Problems of Charities and other Private Institutions with similar Tax Treatment (Congress 1985)

11a. Taxation of domestic shareholders on undistributed income of foreign corporate affiliates: objectives, techniques and consequences (Congress 1986)

11b. International Tax Treatment of Common Law Trusts (Congress 1986)

* Available from Kluwer Law and Taxation Publishers
P.O. Box 23
7400 GA Deventer, The Netherlands
(tel.: +31 5700 47261)

TABLE OF CONTENTS

INTRODUCTION

The international tax treatment of common law trusts raises some important and complex problems. In the first place, the tax treatment of trusts varies widely in those jurisdictions which accept the trust as a domestic legal institution. In some situations the trust is a separate taxpayer. In others the beneficiary or the settlor of the trust is the tax subject. Matters become even more complex when trusts must be considered from the point of view of the tax laws of taxing jurisdictions which do not themselves utilize the legal institution of the trust. There is little published material available on the international taxation of trusts and there have been few attempts to analyze trust taxation on a comparative basis. The Seminar in connection with the 40th IFA Congress in New York has made a substantial contribution to our understanding of this relatively unexplored topic.

The Seminar began with a description by Professor Donald Trautman of the background and history of the common law trust and the International Convention on the Recognition of Trusts. A summary of Professor Trautman's remarks is contained in Part II of these proceedings. Following Mr. Trautman's introductory remarks, the Seminar examined a number of concrete problems and the possible solutions to these problems under the laws of the various countries represented. The problems were structured to begin with basic jurisdictional issues and then to consider a number of increasingly more complex variations. The text of the problems around which the Seminar discussions centered is contained in Part III.

The papers in this collection represent the analysis of the problems by the various panelists. In general, the papers begin with a short description of the overall approach to trust taxation in the jurisdiction in question and then turn to specific answers to the individual problems. In order to save space, the problems are not repeated in each individual presentation. While usually the answers to the problems are self-explanatory, it may be useful for the reader to refer to the specific problems as set forth in Part III in order to fully understand the descriptive material. Following the panelists' papers, Part II provides a summary of the Proceedings prepared by Dr. J.B. Bracewell-Milnes.

Special thanks are due to Ms. Margory Appel for assistance in the preparation of these materials.

Hugh T. Ault
May 1987

I. PROCEEDINGS OF THE SEMINAR

AUSTRALIA

Mr. John King

Problem 1

General Principles

1. As a general rule, under Division 6 of Part III of the Income Tax Assessment Act 1936, as amended, (the 'Act') a trust, though not a legal entity, is taxed as if it were a separate taxpayer. Thus, each year an income tax return form for the trust must be completed and filed, setting forth all the income derived by the trust during the relevant fiscal year and all its deductions, rebates, credits and exemptions. The return must also be accompanied by a balance sheet for the trust as at the end of the fiscal year (or, if there is no balance sheet, a detailed statement of assets and liabilities), a profit and loss statement for the operations of the trust during the relevant year, particulars relating to any provision and reserve accounts of the trust and a reconciliation between the accounting net income of the trust for the relevant year and the net income of the trust for income tax purposes. The Australian federal income tax treatment of the trustee and the beneficiary depends upon the terms of the trust and the additional factors described below.

2. As a general rule (except in the case of so-called corporate unit trusts and so-called public trading trusts, to which special rules apply, and subject to special provisions relating to foreign (i.e. non-Australian) source income derived by the trust), the principle governing the taxation of trusts in Australia is that the whole of the net income of the trust for Australian tax purposes should be liable to tax in the year in which it is derived by the trust. Generally, the income is taxed either to the beneficiaries or to the trustee as follows:

(a) A beneficiary is taxable, under s.97(1)(a), on that part of the trust's net income to which he is 'presently entitled' at the end of the tax year – i.e.,

(i) First, on that part of the net income of the trust for that year which has been paid to him or paid or applied for his benefit during the year: see s.95A(1); and

(*ii*) Secondly, on that part of the net income for the year which has not been paid to him or paid or applied for his benefit but to which he has a vested and indefeasible interest at the end of the year: see s.95A(2). If the beneficiary is presently entitled to such an amount, the actual date of distribution of that amount to him is irrelevant.

If the beneficiary is a resident of Australia at the end of the year of income and is not under a legal disability, the beneficiary is personally assessed. If either the beneficiary is under a legal disability or the beneficiary is not a resident of Australia at the end of the year of income, the trustee is assessed on behalf of the beneficiary and would pay the tax out of the entitlement of the beneficiary.

(*b*) The trustee, on behalf of the trust itself, is liable to tax, generally at a special rate under s.99A, on that part (if any) of the net income of the trust for the year to which no beneficiary is presently entitled at the end of the year of income. This would include an amount of income where it is not possible at the end of the year to determine with certainty who is or will become absolutely entitled to receive the amount. Accordingly, income which is accumulated in the trust is normally income to which no person is presently entitled at the end of the tax year and is therefore taxed to the trustee. Normally, the tax would be paid out of the income to be accumulated and only the net after tax income would be accumulated.

(*c*) Difficult questions can arise where there is a difference between the net income of the trust for accounting purposes and the net income for tax purposes.

3. If part or the whole of any income derived by the trust in any year is taxed to a beneficiary before he receives it or (because no beneficiary is regarded as presently entitled to it at the end of the relevant year of income) to the trustee, the income is not again subject to tax when it is subsequently distributed to the beneficiary or other beneficiaries: see s.99B(2)(c)(ii).

Answers to Specific Questions

Question 1:

The answer to this question depends upon whether it can be said that beneficiary is 'presently entitled' at the end of the year of income to all or any portion of the income derived by the trust during that year. This will depend upon the terms of the trust. In this case, being the sole beneficiary of the trust, beneficiary would probably be regarded as 'presently entitled' at the end of each year too, and would be taxable on, the whole of the trust's net income for that year: see ss.97(1)(a) and 95A. If he is presently entitled to an amount of net income which he has not actually or constructively received by the end of the year, the date of the actual subsequent payment or distribution of that amount to him or for his benefit is irrelevant.

Question 2:

(i) If, by the terms of the trust, all the income is to be distributed currently to beneficiary (and assuming that there is no difference between the net income of the trust for accounting purposes and the net income of the trust for tax purposes), the whole of that income would be taxable to beneficiary: s.97(1)(a). The date of the actual payment or distribution of the net income to him or for his benefit is irrelevant.

(ii) If, by the terms of the trust, all of the income belongs to beneficiary but it is expressly provided that it is not to be paid over to him until a future date, beneficiary would probably nonetheless be deemed, by s.95A(2), to be presently entitled to that income and would therefore now be taxable on it.

The position would be different if the person or persons ultimately entitled to the accumulated income could not be determined until expiration of the period of the accumulation. In that case, in the meantime the income would be regarded as income to which no beneficiary is presently entitled. Australian source income would be taxed to the trustee, generally under s.99A. However, in this case the income would be regarded as having a foreign source. Where and to the extent to which no beneficiary is presently entitled to any foreign source income of the trust at the end of any year of income and, as in this case:

- no trustee of the trust is at any time during the year a resident of Australia, and
- the central management and control of the trust was not in Australia at any time during the year of income

(and therefore the trust is not regarded as a 'resident trust estate': see s.95(2)), the income in question would not be taxed to the trustee. Instead, it would be taxed in the income year it is distributed to any beneficiary if he is a resident of Australia at any time during that year. No Australian tax would be payable on the distribution if, in the year of distribution, the recipient was not a resident of Australia at any time during that year.

(iii) If the discretion relates only to the date of payment of the income to the beneficiary, he would probably nonetheless be regarded as presently entitled to, and would now be immediately taxable on, the whole of the income of the trust: see s.95A(2).

The position would be different if the discretion relates to entitlement and the identity of the person or persons ultimately entitled to any accumulated income could not be determined until the expiration of the period of the accumulation. In that case, beneficiary would only become presently entitled to income of a year when and to the extent to which, before the end of the year, the trustee either irrevocably resolved to distribute income in his favour or paid or applied income to him or for his benefit, whichever first occured: see s.101.

Income of a year to which beneficiary was presently entitled at the end of the year would be taxable to beneficiary as under (i) above. Income of a year to which no beneficiary was presently entitled at the end of the year would be taxable as under (ii) above.

Question 3:

Generally, income derived by a trust during a year of income and to which a beneficiary is presently entitled at the end of the year retains in the hand of the beneficiary the same character that it had in the hands of the trustee – e.g. dividends, interest or other income: see *Syme v. Commissioner of Stamp Duties (Victoria)* (1914) 18 CLR 519, *Baker v. Archer-Shee* [1927] AC 844, *Archer-Shee v. Garland* [1931] AC 212 and *Charles v. Commissioner of Taxation (Australia)* (1954) 90 CLR 598.

There is no case law on the characterization question where income has been accumulated. In practice, if the issue was ever a material one, the answer may be influenced to a substantial degree by the accounting treatment of the accumulated income.

Problem 2

General Principles

1. The Act, s.95(2), provides that a trust shall be taken to be a 'resident trust estate' in relation to a year of income if—

- A trustee of the trust was a resident of Australia at any time during the year of income; or
- The central management and control of the trust was in Australia at any time during the year of income.

2. The general principle is that there is liable to be included:

- In the net income of a 'resident trust estate', the income of the trust from sources within, and also from sources outside Australia;
- In the net income of a trust which does not qualifiy as a 'resident trust estate', only the income of the trust from Australian sources.

In the case of a trust which is not a resident trust estate, the trustee will not be liable to Australian tax on income derived by the trust from sources outside Australia to which no beneficiary is entitled at the end of the year of income, whereas the trustee would be liable to Australian tax on such income if the trust was a resident trust estate during that year of income. Thus, the concept of a 'resident estate' is only relevant to the taxation of foreign (i.e. ex Australian) source income to which no beneficiary is presently entitled at the end of the year of income in which it was derived by the trust. Generally, the distinction between a 'resident trust estate' and a trust estate which is not a 'resident trust estate' is irrelevant for other Australian tax purposes.

Question 1:

(a) Under the test just stated, the mere fact that the creator of the trust is an Australian resident would not cause the trust to be a 'resident trust estate'. As the trust would not meet either of the two criteria stated in s.95(2), mentioned above, either one of which would cause it to be a 'resident trust estate', the trust would not be characterized as a 'resident trust estate' for Australian tax purposes.

(b) The mere fact that the trust was formed under the laws of Australia would also not be sufficient to cause the trust to be characterized as a 'resident trust estate' for Australian tax purposes. This is because neither one of the two criteria stated in s.95(2) is satisfied.

(c) Under s.95(2)(a), the fact that the trustee of the trust was a resident of Australia at some time during the year of income would cause the trust to be characterized as a 'resident trust estate' during that year of income for Australian tax purposes.

(d) The mere fact that beneficiary is an Australian resident would not be sufficient to cause the trust to be characterized as a 'resident trust estate' for Australian tax purposes. This is because neither one of the two criteria stated in s.95(2) is satisfied.

Question 2:

None of the factors mentioned is relevant to the two statutory criteria stated in s.95(2) for determining when a trust is to be characterized as a 'resident trust estate' for Australian tax purposes.

Problem 3

Question 1:

(a) Australian witholding tax is payable in respect of dividends and interest. For the purposes of Australian domestic witholding tax laws, a beneficiary who is 'presently entitled' to a dividend included in the income of a trust estate is deemed to have derived the dividend itself: s.128A(3). As the dividend was originally paid by a corporation that is an Australian resident for Australian tax purposes, and the beneficiary is not an Australian resident and does not carry on business in Australia at or through a permanent establishment in Australia, the beneficiary is liable to Australian tax, at the appropriate withholding tax rate, on the income currently distributed to him, which is deemed to consist of a dividend. Prima facie, tax is payable by him at the rate of 30%. However, for the purposes of the question, it is assumed that the prima facie rate of withholding tax on dividends paid from country A is 25%.

Under most income tax treaties to which Australia is party, this rate is reduced to 15% in the case of dividends to which the treaty applies.

However, generally, income tax treaties to which Australia is a party only give treaty benefits to dividends beneficially derived by residents of the other country which is a party to the treaty: see Articles 10(1) and 10(3) of the USA Agreement; 8(3) and 8(4)(b) of the United Kingdom Agreement (as substituted by the December 7, 1967 protocol); 9(1) and 9(3) of the French Agreement; and 10(1) and 10(3) of the Swiss Agreement. Contrast Article 10(1) of the Federal Republic of Germany Agreement, which applies the reduced rate to dividends paid to a resident of the Federal Republic and does not refer to the beneficial entitlement to the dividends.

However, if the address of the trustee of the trust is shown in the register of members of the paying company as in a country with which Australia has an income tax treaty and the company pays the dividend to the trustee, the statutory provisions, Act sections 221YK–221YR, and relevant income tax regulations, Regs. 54ZF-ZK, only oblige the paying company to deduct withholding tax on the basis of the residence of the trustee, and do not require it to have any regard to the beneficial entitlement to the dividend.

Accordingly, in the present case, the paying company would only be obliged to deduct withholding tax at the rate of 15% from the dividend which it pays to the trustee, even it is aware of the entitlement of beneficiary. Beneficiary is liable to tax at the rate of 30% (with credit being given for the 15% already deducted) but the trustee would not normally be obliged to deduct or pay the balance of the tax due. In practice, it seems that the Australian Taxation Office makes no attempt to recover any additional tax due by beneficiary in these circumstances.

(b) If beneficiary is not 'presently entitled' to the dividend income which is not currently distributed to him, the withholding tax rate would be determined solely by reference to the status of the trustee, being the recipient of the dividends. In that case, as the trustee would not be beneficially entitled to the dividends it received, generally it would not be entitled to claim the treaty benefit of a reduced withholding tax rate.

However, if the address of the trustee is shown in the register of members of the paying company as in a country with which Australia has an income tax treaty and the company pays the dividend to the trustee, the statutory provisions and relevant income tax regulations only oblige the paying company to deduct withholding tax on the basis of the residence of the trustee, and do not require it to have any regard to the beneficial entitlement to the dividend.

Accordingly, in the present case, the paying company would only be obliged to deduct withholding tax at the rate of 15% from the dividend which it pays to the trustee, even if it is aware that, by reason of its non beneficial interest in the dividend, the trustee may not be entitled to the benefit of a reduced treaty withholding tax rate. The trustee is however personally liable to tax at the rate of 30% (with credit being given for the 15% already deducted). In practice, it seems that the Australian Taxation Office makes no attempt to recover any additional tax due by a trustee in these circumstances.

(c) As for (a) above in relation to income currently distributed to beneficiary. As for (b) above in relation to income not currently distributed.

Question 2:

(a) If the treaty between Australia and Country C gives treaty benefits to dividends beneficially derived by residents of Country C, beneficiary would be entitled to the reduced withholding tax rate of 15%.

However, under the relevant statutory provisions and income tax regulations, if the address of the trustee of the trust is shown in the register of members of the paying company as in Country B, with which Australia does not have an income tax treaty, and the company pays the dividend to the trustee, the paying company is obliged to deduct withholding tax at the full rate and do not entitle it to have any regard to beneficial entitlement.

In practice, it would nonetheless be open to beneficiary and the trustee to provide evidence to the Australian Taxation Office as to the entitlement of beneficiary to the benefit of the reduced treaty rate and, if given a private letter ruling to that effect by the Taxation office, to furnish the ruling to the paying company and request it to withhold tax at the lower rate.

If tax had been deducted by the paying company at the full rate, beneficiary would be required to claim a refund for the excess withholding tax.

(b) If beneficiary is not 'presently entitled' to the dividend income which is not currently distributed to him, the withholding tax rate would be determined solely by reference to the status of the trustee, being the recipient of the dividends. In that case, as there is no tax treaty with the country of residence of the trustee, Country B, withholding tax at the full tax rate of 25% would be payable.

(c) As for (a) above in relation to income currently distributed to beneficiary. As for (b) above in relation to income not currently distributed.

Question 3:

(a) See 2(a) above.
(b) See 2 above.

Problem 4

Question 1:

1. Pre July 1, 1987 Law:

Under prior law (which ceased to apply on July 1, 1987), beneficiary was deemed to have derived dividends equal to the grossed up amount of that amount of the net income of the trust to which he is 'presently entitled' at the end of each year of income: i.e. the aggregrate of the net amount to which he is presently entitled and the withholding tax referrable to that amount: see s.6B and note that s.23(q) is inapplicable to the amounts attributable to dividends. Beneficiary would be entitled to claim a credit under s.45(1A) for the amount of withholding tax referrable to that amount of the dividend income of the trust to which he is 'presently entitled'.

Post July 1, 1987 Law:

From July 1, 1987, a general worldwide foreign tax credit system will commence to apply in Australia. As from that date, different statutory provisions will apply. However, in the case of income attributable to dividends, the result is the same under both present law and the new foreign tax credit system: s.6AC will effect the grossing up, s.6AB will deem beneficiary to have been personally liable for, and to have paid, the withholding tax, and s.160AF will entitle the taxpayer to claim a credit for the tax which he is deemed to have paid.

Question 2:

The source of the income is not relevant for foreign tax credit purposes under either the present law or the new foreign tax credit system to apply from July 1, 1987.

Question 3:

Under prior law, the credit available under s.45(1A) was limited to tax payable under the laws of the country of residence of the company paying the dividends, namely Country A. Accordingly, credit will not be available for the tax imposed by Country B.

Under the new foreign tax credit system to apply from July 1, 1987, credit will be available for the tax imposed by Country B: under s.6AB the foreign tax, for which beneficiary is entitled to a credit under s.160AF, would include any foreign tax paid by any person, either directly or by deduction, in respect of the dividends.

Problem 5

Question 1:

As for Problem 1, the existence of the power of the Creator to revoke the trust has no effect on the tax position of beneficiary provided that any entitlement of beneficiary to any income not yet paid to him or for his benefit cannot be revoked (and assuming that any payment already made to, or for the benefit of, beneficiary cannot subsequently be reversed). An anti-avoidance provision (s.102) does not apply because the Creator is not a resident of Australia and the income is attributable to sources out of Australia.

As for Problem 2, the existence of the power is irrelevant to the residence of the trust.

As for Problem 3, a special withholding tax provision (s.128B(3)(e)) does not apply because the principal anti-avoidance provision (s.102) is inapplicable.

As for Problem 4, the analysis used with regard to Problem 1 would apply.

Question 2:

Generally, whenever a beneficiary has the power to require the trust assets to be transferred to him in whole or part, he would be regarded as 'presently entitled' to the whole of the income of trust.

In the case of Problem 1, as beneficiary can require all the trust assets to be transferred to him, he would always be regarded as 'presently entitled' to, and would be taxable on, the whole of the income of the trust.

As for Problem 2, the existence of the power is irrelevant to the residence of the trust.

As for Problem 3, for the reasons stated above in relation to Problem 1, beneficiary would be regarded as 'presently entitled' to the dividend income. Therefore, in relation to Problem 3: the answers to Questions 1(a), (b) and (c) are in each case as shown for Questions 1(a) and the answers to Question 2(a), (b) and (c) are in each case as shown for Question 2(a).

As for Problem 4, the same analysis used with regard to Problem 1 would apply.

FRANCE

Mr. François Tripet

ANGLO-SAXON TRUSTS AND FRENCH INCOME TAX LAW

French tax legislation is characterized by an almost complete lack of statutory provisions or official comments on the institution of the trust, which never fails to strike the observer who knows that the French tax-payers abroad covered by a trust, the English-speaking citizens living in our country who are founders or beneficiaries of a trust, together with the generations of French citizens in FRANCE benefitting by trusts set up by their elders amount to several tens of thousands of taxpayers. Apart from section 120–9e of the General Tax Code, which treats the income from a trust as the income from a security, and an administrative circular dated 25 March 1981 containing 49 lines of comments on the Franco-American tax convention of 28 July 1967, which is laconic to say the least, the tax expert, whether a theorist or a practitioner, has no specifically fiscal principles to fall back on.

Nevertheless, the French tax specialist is not lacking in guide lines when attempting a comprehensive fiscal analysis of the institution of the trust since tax law is based on legal concepts taken over direct from civil law, unless otherwise stipulated in the tax regulations.

The following comments and analyses relate only to family trusts. In other words, they do not deal with business trusts, financial trusts, voting trusts, investment trusts, pension trusts, charitable trusts, trusts for liquidation and other instruments designed for the needs of a particular trade, business or profession. Where income tax is concerned, the trust raises five main issues: its separate fiscal existence, its fiscal residence, the nature of the sums distributed, the grounds for the taxation of the beneficiaries, and the ability to rely on international tax conventions.

a) Separate fiscal existance

Since a trust has no legal personality, one might be tempted to conclude that its fiscal personality is extremely volatile. This is in fact the approach of American tax law. A trust is treated as a separate tax-payer whenever it is clearly outside the control of the settlor i.e. the latter no longer has the power to revoke the trust or to supervise closely the trustee's management or the right to be the only or the principal beneficiary. As a separate tax-payer, the trust pays tax on the income collected by the trustee, but when this income is distributed to the beneficiaries, the latter receive a tax credit corresponding to the tax already paid by the trust.

If, on the other hand, the settlor's control over the trust remains apparent, the settlor is deemed to be still in possession of the assets placed in the trust. In such a case e.g. that of the Grantor trust, the trust is held to be non-existent for fiscal purposes and the taxation on the income collected by the trustee is levied on the settlor direct.

In its administrative circular dated 25 March 1981 (BODGI No.59 of 25 March 1981, 14 B–2–81) dealing with American trusts from the standpoint of the Franco-American tax convention, the General Tax Directorate readily endorses this approach. In practice, therefore, it tends to treat any revocable trust as non-existent and to recognise the separate legal personality only of the irrevocable trusts. It is worth asking whether it would not be worth adopting a more flexible position by distinguishing between three cases:

1) Settlor and beneficiary are one and the same person

Here, it seems logical to treat the trust as non-existent for tax purposes. The settlor is taxed on the income collected by the trustee in respect of the year in which the trustee is credited with the said income (irrespective of whether or not it is actually distributed to the settlor/beneficiary).

2) Settlor and beneficiary are two separate persons

Here, it does not matter whether the trust is revocable or not; only the beneficiary is liable for tax on the income actually distributed to him by the trustee. However, two exceptions can be envisaged, but only in the case of revocable trusts:

– if it is clear that the settlor, being liable for tax in the higher brackets, has put the assets in trust solely for the purpose of paying income to a beneficiary who is a close relation or friend liable for tax in a much lower bracket, it is incumbent on the tax authorities to prove the settlor's intention to evade tax and accordingly to petition the court to declare the trust non-existent for tax purposes.

– if it also clear that, through a revocable trust, the trustee (assumed to have discretionary power over the distribution) is pursuing a policy of accumulating income and systematically only paying it out to the beneficiary with respect to years in which he is liable for much less tax, it is incumbent on the tax authorities to prove that the principal purpose of the trust arrangement was to evade the progressive character of the tax and to petition the court accordingly to declare the trust non-existent for tax purposes or alternatively to declare that the policy of accumulating income is non-demurrable.

3) *The settlor is one beneficiary among others*

In this case, the trust does not exist for tax purposes. However, the consequences of this existence may be annulled by the courts in the case of a revocable trust in respect and only in respect of any distribution made to the settlor if it is clear that such an arrangement is not warranted for other than predominantly tax purposes. Similarly, the tax authorities would be entitled, with a view to preventing abuse of the law, to inquire whether the distribution of income to other beneficiaries or the policy of accumulating income is not in fact mainly designed to place the settlor's income in the hands of relatives or friends or systematically to escape the progressive impact of the income tax.

To sum up, it would surely be over-hasty as well as legally unjustified to treat revocable trusts as non-existent for tax purposes. If such were the case, the arrangements of morally irreproachable trusts would lead to settlors being taxed on income they have not received and to beneficiaries being exempted in respect of income they have received, which would probably result in frauds of a new type.

A fairer approach would be to treat as non-existent for tax purposes a revocable trust demonstrably set up for the primary purpose of evading tax (apart, of course, from cases in which settlor and beneficiary are one and the same person, when the non-existence of the trust for tax purposes is automatic). As regards irrevocable trusts, there is no need to underscore the fact that they are unanimously agreed to possess separate personality for tax purposes.

It goes without saying, of course, that the trustee himself is never liable for tax on the income he collects on behalf of the trust. On the other hand, he is responsible for making the trust pay the tax for which it is liable if its separate existence for tax purposes is recognised.

b) Nature of the sums distributed by the trustee

As French tax law now stands (section 120–9e of the General Tax Code), any 'product' distributed by a trustee is deemed to be an income derived from securities. This provision is ambiguous (since an income from securities may equally well be a dividend or a payment of interest) and indefensible since distributions of capital by the trustee are liable to income tax.

For this reason, the administrative circular of 25 March 1981, mentioned earlier, issued as a result of the Franco-American tax convention, lays down the principle of consistency, without realising that this common-sense principle is liable to raise more problems than it solves.

The consistency rule means that any income collected by a trustee on behalf of a trust is not modified by its passage through the trust fund and retains its character when distributed to the beneficiaries. For example, property earnings or dividends collected by the trustee remain property earnings or dividends in the hands of the beneficiary when distributed to him.

This is a direct application of the fundamental legal principle that a trust does not possess a separate legal personality. This clearly distinguishes it from the contract setting up a capital investment company, which has a separate legal personality converting, unless otherwise stated, a large variety of upstream incomes into a single downstream income – the dividend.

The operation of this principle in practice does not raise any particular problems in the case of the strict trusts i.e. trusts distributing incomes to beneficiaries as and when they are collected by the trustee.

On the other hand, in the case of a discretionary or complex trust, the trustee may accumulate the income (sometimes over a long period), collect the income on this income, and even incorporate it wholly or partly in the capital. This means that he has to maintain very careful accounts enabling him not only to distinguish between capital and income (which is compulsory) but also to identify clearly the income on this income (usually dividends or interest) and even any capital gains arising out of the investment of this income or the income thereon.

However, the legal autonomy of a trust does not always make it possible to impose such stringent accounting and technical requirements on the trustee.

What happens then in the case of a 'sum' distributed to a beneficiary several years later and made up of components which it is often difficult to identify clearly?

The author of this article submitted a practical aproach to the General

Tax Directorate in 1982, which, in the absence of anything better, appears to be still employed:

1) The case of a trustee maintaining careful general and analytical accounts

In this case, the identification of the income by nature, by origin and by year, and the identification of its subsequent yields or re-employment makes it easy for the beneficiary to find out how the sum distributed to him is composed: the consistency rule applies throughout, provided the trustee not only certifies the nature of each component but is also a professional subject to rules of third party liability akin to those imposed on the regulated professions in France (bankers, insurers, accountants, notaries, lawyers, legal and tax advisers etc.).

However, in view of the rule in French case law to the effect that an income is a sum from a source that can be renewed, it was proposed that any income accumulated by the trustee over a period of more than five years should be treated as a distribution of capital and added to the capital of the trust, it being clear that in any event, the sums distributed to the beneficiaries on the winding up of a trust are, depending on circumstances, treated as capital or income, depending on the financial records placed before the court when the trust goes into liquidation.

2) The case of a trustee maintaining accounts which do not make it possible to distinguish between capital and income (a very improbable case) or the different types of capital accumulated

– while the trust is in operation, any sums paid to the beneficiary which involve a capital disinvestment proved to be such by the trustee are deemed to be capital. The surplus distributed (if any) is treated as a dividend.

– when the trust is wound up, unless shown to be otherwise by the financial records submitted to the court, any distributions to the beneficiaries are treated as capital in so far as it can be proved (at least in general terms) that the accumulated and current income has already been distributed (an extrapolation of the principle involved in section 112–1e of the General Tax Code).

In the absence of proof, it is to be feared that the whole distribution will be treated as the payment of a dividend. Lastly, the question arises whether section 120–9e of the General Tax Code (already inapplicable in practice to US and Canadian trusts) is liable to become inapplicable as well to any type of non-US trust.

The practice of the General Tax Directorate appears to meet this concern adequately, at least in so far as this provision is not used as a means of levying income tax on proved distributions of capital.

To prevent any ambiguities, the reform or even the rescission of section 120–9e of the General Tax Code might be proposed.

c) Fact entailing taxation of beneficiaries

The question arises whether the beneficiary should be taxed with respect to the year during which the income is actually distributed to him by the trustee or with respect to the year in which an income is credited to the trustee on behalf of the trust.

The administrative circular dated 25 March 1981, mentioned earlier, clearly lays down, in the case of US trusts, the principle that the beneficiary must be taxed at the time when the income is actually distributed by the trustee.

On grounds of common-sense, this rule should surely be extended to cover all non-US trusts.

Nevertheless, the converse will apply if the trust does not exist for tax purposes for obvious reasons (one in which settlor and beneficiary are one and the same person) or if the trust does not exist for tax purposes for reasons advanced to that end (cases of legal abuse referred to in a) above).

d) Fiscal residence of the trust

Deciding on the fiscal residence of the trust is very important when it becomes necessary, at the international level, to define the territorial source of an income and the ability of a trust to avail itself of bilateral tax conventions, which of course only benefit one or other resident of each contracting State. The legal approach to the question is based on French case law, which assumes the residence of a trust to be the same as that of its law of autonomy i.e. the law to which the parties to the trust have agreed to subject it.

For example, a trust under Bahamian law would be resident in the BAHAMAS and a trust under Irish law would be resident in IRELAND. This approach has the merit of legal consistency but it quickly proves to be impracticable when the trustee, the place from which the trust's assets are managed, the residence of the settlor and that of the beneficiary or beneficiaries are concentrated in another country or dispersed among several countries.

Basing oneself on the philosophy underlying Article 7 of the Hague International Convention of 20 October 1984, relating to the determination of the implicit law with which the trust has the closest links (the 'closely connected rule'), it is surely possible to propose a more realistic and pragmatic approach, using successive criteria for determining residence:

– the first criterion should be the place from which the trust is managed,

– the subsidiary criterion should be location of the trust's assets,

– the next criterion should be the trustee's place of residence or establishment,

– the last criterion should be the purposes of the trust and the places where they are to be achieved.

Taking these criteria in conjunction, it will be found that the trust is first and foremost resident in the country where the trustee is located, from which he manages the assets and perhaps where the assets are themselves located. There is considerable geographical homogeneity between the trustee, the assets of the trust and the machinery of management, if only because of the heavy responsibilities borne by the trustee.

In point of fact, the question of a trust's residence only requires careful investigation on the case of trusts set up under the law of a country coming under the heading of a 'tax haven'. It can readily be decided that they are not residents of the tax haven if the country in question simply acts as a deposit for the deed of trust and acts as the trustee's place of residence. They are much more likely to be residents of the country if the management and assets of the trust are both situated there, with emphasis being placed on the first criterion in the event of a geographical distinction between the location of the management and the location of the assets.

This approach is compatible with the specific law of the international tax conventions: in the great majority of cases, these conventions define the residence of persons 'other than natural persons' by reference to their actual place of management. In the special case of the Franco-Canadian tax convention of 2 May 1975, it is even stipulated that a trust is deemed to be a fiscal resident of CANADA if, and only if, the trustee is himself a fiscal resident of CANADA (combined effect of articles 3–1-b and 4–1 of the Convention and Canadian domestic tax law).

Nevertheless, the determination of the fiscal residence of a trust primarily on the basis of the trustee's fiscal residence or the trust's actual place of management must not be allowed to obscure the difficulty that would arise if there were two co-trustees (as occurs more and more frequently) or if there is a corporate trustee (an investment company acting as trustee) with a board of directors characterised by a geographically dispersed membership.

In cases like these, the French tax authorities tend to await the reaction of tax authorities in other countries faced with the same question before deciding on their attitude, with the result that some trusts find themselves in the uncomfortable position of being completely non-resident for tax purposes for years on end and in the meantime are unable to claim the benefit from any international tax convention.

It is essential, therefore, nowadays, in order to rule out any such major tax problems, to include in the trust deed itself an article dealing specifically with the 'residence' of the trust whenever the trust arrangement – having regard to the parties thereto and its purposes – is quite liable to involve a wide geographical dispersal of the trust's component parts.

In this discussion, it is impossible to ignore the line of least resistance taken by many tax authorities – not excluding those in France – whereby they determine the fiscal residence of a trust by reference to the country in which it pays most taxes; this attitude is based on the asumption that the parties to a trust paying a significant volume of taxes in a given country have every interest – since they have to make a fiscal contribution – in taking advantage of the tax reliefs which the said country may afford them, so that the involvement of the various components of the trust becomes even more pronounced.

This attitude is somewhat pernicious because it tends to accept the widespread assumption that the parties enter into a trust arrangement mainly for fiscal reasons. Nothing could be further from the truth, not only because of the tax legislation which, in the main English-speaking countries, has progressively whittled away the exorbitant tax advantages possessed by the trusts during the first half of the XXth century, but above all because of the seriousness and finality of the dismemberment of ownership involved in setting up a trust, which rarely impels an owner to become a settlor for essentially fiscal reasons. It is, for example, enlightening to note that most of the literature issued by the leading trust banks in the tax havens to vaunt the merits of their specialist departments never refers to the alleged tax advantages but instead emphasises flexibility of management and promptness of judicial supervision, which are sometimes lacking in the courts of the main English-speaking countries.

A final point concerns the fiscal residence of a trust when the latter is deemed to be non-existent for tax purposes or is asserted to be so. The point might appear to be academic since the taxation of the trust's income is levied directly on the settlor and in some cases involving abuse, on the beneficiaries. In fact, however, the point remains entirely valid in the case of income the nature and territorial source of which are unidentified.

Let us take the case of a revocable discretionary trust under Bermudan law which is deemed to be a fiscal resident of the United States in that it is actually managed from New York. This trust may have accumulated dividends and interest from several countries not linked to FRANCE by a tax convention but linked to the UNITED STATES by a tax convention.

Let us assume that the settlor and sole beneficiary of the trust is a person who has become a French resident for tax purposes. The fact that the trust does not exist for tax purposes means that the settlor-beneficiary will have to pay tax on any dividends deemed to be from an 'American source' i.e. subject to a withholding tax of 15% in the UNITED STATES and entitled to an equal tax credit in FRANCE. The trust being deemed to be a resident of the UNITED STATES, any distributions by the trust are deemed to be from American sources and are covered by the provisions of the Franco-American tax convention of 1967.

On the other hand, if the trust – although non-existent as a separate tax-payer – had not been treated as a UNITED STATES resident, not only would it not have been possible to set off the deductions made by the countries in which the incomes originated against the US tax payable by the trust, but in addition FRANCE would not have granted a tax credit in respect of income already taxed in countries not linked with FRANCE by a tax convention.

In our example, it is assumed that the UNITED STATES does not argue from the non-existence of the trust for tax purposes that its residence is that of its settlor-beneficiary, as would appear to be the position under its case law (cf BW JONES TRUST '46 BTA 531, aff'd, 132 F 2d 914, 4th cir. 1943; REV.RUL. 64–307, 1964–2 C.B 163; REV.RUL. 62–154, 1962–2 C.B 148) and that of several other leading English-speaking countries.

e) The application of international tax conventions

The ability to avail oneself of the provisions of an international tax convention depends on whether one can be considered to be a resident of one or other of the contracting States within the meaning of the said Convention. This point is discussed in the previous section and we saw that in principle, a trust – whether a separate taxpayer or not – is deemed to be a resident of the country with which it has the closest links i.e. of the place from which it is actually managed, which is usually the same as the place where the trustee is established and, in any event, the place where the trust's assets are located.

The conclusion to be drawn therefrom is that the income derived from third countries which have no convention with FRANCE becomes income deemed to be covered by a convention if the trust is resident in a country linked with FRANCE by a tax convention. The converse conclusion must also be drawn that the incomes from a source covered by a convention forfeit this status if they pass through a trust deemed to be resident in a country not linked to FRANCE by a tax convention, which may have very harsh fiscal consequences: for example, an American property income (exempt in FRANCE under the Franco-American convention) passing through a trust resident in the Netherlands Antilles, becomes liable to tax at full rate in FRANCE irrespective of the tax already paid in the UNITED STATES. In other words, one goes from exemption to double taxation!

The final conclusion to be drawn is that in the case of a trust resident in a country party to a convention with incomes from a French source and distributed to a beneficiary resident in a country not linked with France by a tax convention, FRANCE must grant the benefits applicable under the convention linking it with the trust's country of residence and cannot refuse them on the ground that the income would accrue to a beneficiary who is not himself covered by any tax convention with FRANCE. In this connection, it might be noted that there is sometimes an unfortunate discrepancy between law and practice, since the French tax authorities refuse to grant the benefits provided for in the convention linking FRANCE with the trust's country of residence without proof that the beneficiary will in fact pay tax in his country of residence on the income distributed to him by the trustee. This attitude is surely justified whenever the beneficiary indulges in 'treaty shopping' i.e. has made undue use of the advantages conferred by international tax conventions. At the same time, the French tax authorities must not evade their responsibility to prove that this undue use is a constant factor in the case.

Lastly, the question arises whether, in the case of the beneficiary (assumed to be tax resident of FRANCE), the tax paid by the trust forms a credit that can be set off against the payments made to him by the trustee.

FRANCE does not recognise the principle of the underlying tax credit, only that of the direct tax credit.

This is pointed out in the administrative circular of 25 March 1981 mentioned earlier, dealing with the case of the Franco-American convention but in practice applicable to all situations covered by conventions. When the trust is a separate tax-payer and pays tax on the income the trustee has collected, this tax does not form a tax credit from the beneficiary's standpoint when he actually receives the income distributed to him by the trustee: the only tax credit possessed by the beneficiary is constituted by the tax paid by him at the time when the income is distributed to him.

A fortiori, the conclusion must be drawn that the tax paid on the income from a third country and collected by the trustee, even if it can constitute a tax credit when the trust is taxed as a separate tax-payer, cannot once more form a tax credit in the case of the beneficiary at the time when the income in question is distributed to him (i.e. there is no underlying tax credit). However, there is nothing to stop the French Government accepting codicils to existing tax conventions specifically providing for underlying tax credits to be taken into account.

f) The special case of Canadian trusts

When the Franco-Canadian tax convention of 1975 was being negotiated, the representatives of CANADA requested the inclusion in the convention of special provisions relating to trusts. These were the first of their kind, and it may well be wondered whether in some respects they may not constitute a precedent in any similar negotiations between FRANCE and other national authorities over codicils to existing conventions.

1. The question of the *residence of the trust for tax purposes* is clearly settled as follows: any trust under Canadian law is deemed to be a resident of CANADA for tax purposes if it is treated as a Canadian resident for tax purposes (article 3–1-B of the treaty) under the domestic tax legislation of CANADA. In other words, this clause leaves it to domestic law to decide whether or not a trust is resident for the purposes of the convention. It so happens that at the present time, a trust is a resident of CANADA for tax purposes if the trustee himself is a resident of the country for tax purposes. But it should not be concluded from this that the question of the trust's residence for tax purposes is simply that of the trustee, since Canadian domestic law may one day be amended to suit other criteria or a combination of criteria.

On the other hand, it is clear that the principle that the residence of a trust for the purposes of a convention may be settled by the law of the country of its establishment has now been laid down and may constitute a precedent. In practice, it is already apparent that this principle is applied in Franco-American cases: for example, the General Tax Directorate tends to admit that a trust under Bermudan law is a resident of BERMUDA for tax purposes if Bermudan domestic law recognises it as such (the trust being thereby excluded from coverage by the Franco-American convention). On the other hand, if Bermudan domestic law recognises a given trust as non-resident for tax purposes, or is silent on this aspect and if, *in addition,* the involvement of components of the trust on American territory means that it is a resident of the UNITED STATES for tax purposes under the domestic tax law of that country, then in practice, such a trust is deemed to be a tax resident of the UNITED STATES for the purposes of the Franco-American tax convention.

2. The question of the *definition of the source of the income* of the trust is likewise settled by article 23–3 of the Franco-Canadian treaty, which stipulates that any income or earnings by a resident of FRANCE which have been taxed in CANADA are to be treated as income or earnings from a Canadian source. Taking this general provision in conjunction with article 3-1-B, mentioned earlier, and article 21–2 (providing for a deduction of 15% from any trust income distributed to a resident of FRANCE), one can conclude that any income distributed by a Canadian trust which has been taxed in CANADA is an income deemed to be from a Canadian source: as a result, any income collected by the trustee from third countries (including tax havens) is reclassified as being 'from Canadian sources'.

The Canadian trust, in short, forms a treaty-based screen with respect to third countries from which its income may derive (it should be added, however, that the Franco-Canadian treaty does not contain any clause dealing with abuse of treaty facilities). Should this provision be elevated to the status of a 'precedent' applying to other trusts e.g. British, American, Australian, Singaporean etc. . .?

The reply depends on circumstances:

– if there is an applicable convention between FRANCE and the trust's country of residence for tax purposes containing a provision of the type embodied in article 23–3 of the Franco-Canadian convention (i.e. income from all sources is taxed or taxable by the trust's country of residence for tax purposes), the same conclusions can be accepted as in the case of the Franco-Canadian arrangement.

– if there is no applicable convention between FRANCE and the trust's country of residence for tax purposes, such an extrapolation is not possible, but the practical importance of the question is slight. For example, a trust in the NETHERLANDS ANTILLES receiving an income from American real estate and redistributing it to a French beneficiary will be deemed to be distributing an income from an American source taxable as a dividend from the NETHERLANDS ANTILLES (by virtue of section 120–9e of the General Tax Code).

3. The question of the *determination of the nature of the income* from the trust is settled indirectly by a combination of several provisions of the Franco-Canadian tax treaty and more particularly by article 21–2 (on distributions of income as opposed to distributions of capital) and article 13–1-C (on trusts with a preponderance of real estate), the conclusion being that the sums distributed by a Canadian trust retain the character they possessed when collected by the trustee i.e. dividends, interest, property revenues etc., as the case may be.

Thus, the ruling in section 120–9e of the General Tax Code that any distribution of the yield of a trust constitutes a dividend is clearly set aside by the Franco-Canadian convention. This principle formed a precedent to some extent since six years later, as a result of the Franco-American convention, the General Tax Directorate endorsed the same interpretation in the case of American trusts (administrative circular of 25 March 1981).

4. Lastly, the Franco-Canadian convention contains a number of *novel provisions* concerning *trusts with a preponderance of real estate* and *substantial assignments of trust rights.*

Section 13–1-C states that a Canadian trust possessing mainly real estate assets located in CANADA is deemed, for the purposes of taxation on earnings and capital gains, to be exclusively taxable in CANADA. Conversely, a Canadian trust primarily holding real estate assets located in FRANCE is deemed to be taxable in FRANCE alone for the purposes of the same taxes.

Although the question is not clearly settled, one of the results is that the capital gains of Canadian trust with a preponderance of Canadian real estate distributed to a beneficiary who is a resident of FRANCE for tax purposes are exempt from tax as far as he is concerned (otherwise the provision in the convention would not make sense).

On the other hand, the capital gains of a Canadian trust with a preponderance of French real estate are taxable in FRANCE at the time when they accrue, the tax being paid by the trustee, but are tax-exempt when later distributed to a beneficiary who is a resident of FRANCE for tax purposes (otherwise, there would be double taxation, which would be contrary to the convention).

One can appreciate the economic and fiscal reasons which led the authorities of the two countries to make this novel arrangement. Nevertheless, it is hard to avoid the thought that fiscal realism sometimes has dangerous results: on the French side, for example, it was necessary to take account of section 150-A-bis of the General Tax Code relating to predominantly real estate *companies.*

A trust, however, can in no circumstances be a company since it does not possess legal personality.

It would be a mistake therefore to go any further in the direction of subjecting trusts to the same taxation as companies, as it would lead us to preposterous conclusions; there should, rather, be *special* provision for trusts, even if their fiscal treatment is akin on individual points to that of companies.

Article 13–3-B of the convention is even more disturbing in this respect. It states that the gains made by a beneficiary who is a resident of FRANCE for tax purposes through the transfer or assignment of 25% or more of his rights in a Canadian trust (other than a preponderantly real estate trust) are exclusively taxable in CANADA at a rate not exceeding 25%, unless the beneficiary residing in FRANCE is a Canadian citizen or has been a resident of CANADA for not less than 10 years of his life before the assignment or transfer and a resident of CANADA at any time during the five years preceding the assignment or transfer, in which case, he is treated as if he were a resident of CANADA for tax purposes who had carried out the assignment or transfer in question. One can appreciate the objective of the Canadian authorities: to prevent Canadian residents or citizens from finding it too easy to settle in FRANCE in order to benefit from favourable taxation on their Canadian trust rights.

The French authorities, for their part, accepted this clause because it fitted in with the philosophy underlying section 160 of the General Tax Code concerning transfers of controlling holdings in *companies*.

It is however unfortunate and dangerous that the word trust should have been used in this provision of the convention, which is in fact concerned with companies acting as trusts or with trusts that can be deemed to be companies.

The law of trust – when it does not actually forbid it – displays the utmost reluctance to allow a beneficiary to assign or transfer the property from which he benefits. As a general rule, he can only accept it and defend it or forgo it. It is important therefore that these two novel provisions of the Franco-Canadian tax convention should not be used as a pretext for intellectual exercises designed to place trusts and companies on the same footing.

The general opinion that can be expressed on the Franco-Canadian tax convention is that it is a first experimental approach towards the international tax treatment of trusts by civil law country and a country combining common law and civil law (Quebec) traditions, some provisions of which may serve as 'precedents' (the question of the residence of the trust for tax purposes, and the definition of the source of the trust's income and its nature), whereas other provisions have a precise, limited fiscal purpose.

FEDERAL REPUBLIC OF GERMANY

Mr. Jürgen Killius

Introductory Remarks

As German civil law does not know the common law trust concept, it is understandable that there are no specific provisions in German tax law which deal with the tax treatment of grantors, trustees and beneficiaries. Furthermore, most of the cases reported concern testamentary trusts where the testator was a national and/or resident of a common law jurisdiction, and where the trust funds as well as the trust were located in a common law country. Finally, most of the cases reported relate to the inheritance tax aspects and very few deal with income tax or wealth tax aspects. This explains the uncertainty which still prevails in this area of German tax law which is reflected in our responses below to the questions put in the set of five problems.

The following is a brief summary of the considerations which are pertinent under German tax law in determining the tax aspects of a trust, its grantor, trustees and/or beneficiaries:

1. A revocable trust poses the least problems as it can be assimilated to a contractual trust arrangement *(Treuhandvertrag)* under German civil law for purposes of German tax law as well. We have taken this position in numerous cases and opinions and, in our experience, this view is shared by the tax administration even though there seem to be few authorities in point. See Ratjen, DB 1982, 1793 at 1795. Under section 39(2)(1) General Tax Code – *Abgabenordnung* (AO), the income collected by a trustee *(Treuhänder)* under a German-type trust arrangement is attributed currently to the grantor and this should mean that the character and source of the income collected by the trustee remains unchanged and is likewise attributed to the grantor.

2. The status of irrevocable trusts is more uncertain as there is no tax case as yet which concerns an irrevocable inter-vivos trust and which determines whether a trust can be assimilated to a family foundation *(Familienstiftung)* or some other type of incorporated entity for purposes of German taxation or whether the assets of the trust or the income realized by the trust can be attributed to the beneficiary for purposes of German income taxation. Section 15 of the Foreign Tax Act – *Aussensteuergesetz* (AStG), provides for the current attribution of the income of a foreign family foundation to the creator if and for so long as he is a resident for German tax purposes and thereafter to the German-resident beneficiaries on a pro-rata basis. In this context a family foundation is defined to cover foundations where the grantor, the members of his family and their descendents are entitled to receive more than one half of the income or of the liquidation proceeds. Nevertheless, it is doubtful whether this provision can be applied only if the creator or the beneficiary has a legal claim against the foundation or whether expectancy would suffice. Under a predecessor provision, the prevailing view in literature would have considered a mere expectancy as sufficient and there is no case law reported. Cf. Flick/Wassermeyer/Becker, Commentary to the AStG, annotations 31 *et seq.* to Section 15 AStG.

3. If the intervivos trust should be considered the equivalent of a family foundation (see Raedler-Raupach, *Deutsche Steuern bei Auslandsbeziehungen,* Munich 1966, p. 517) or another form of unincorporated entity (BFH decision of May 31, 1961, BStBl. 1961 III 312; BFH decision of May 29, 1984, DB 1984, 2175), then the place of its registered seat or its principal place of management may determine whether the trust itself could be considered a resident for German income tax purposes. Under Section 1(1)(5) Corporate Income Tax Act – *Körperschaftssteuergesetz* (KStG), such entities are considered resident if they maintain either their registered seat or their principal place of management in Germany. An entity organized under German law has to have its registered seat in Germany; it is, therefore, always a resident taxpayer but this is moot for a common law trust. Furthermore, a resident trustee might create a principal place of management in Germany and thus expose the trust to German income taxation, and for this reason the appointment of German resident trustees should be discouraged.

4. The case law concerning the income tax status of distributions by testamentary trusts is conflicting. In a case handed down by the Tax Court Hannover on October 23, 1964, EFG 1965, 225, the court did not discuss the character of the trust at all but held that the income distributed to the German-resident benficiary constituted other periodical or recurrent income under Section 22 (1) Income Tax Act – *Einkommensteuergesetz* (EStG). On appeal, the *Bundesfinanzhof* (BFH) reversed the decision because it felt that under the circumstances the income distributed by the trust could not be considered periodical or recurrent income; the BFH did not discuss the character of a trust either. These decisions imply, nevertheless, that income flowing through a trust does not retain its characteristics as dividend or interest income. BFH decision of July 20, 1971, BStBl. 1972 II 170. On the other hand, the Tax Court Berlin, in a decision of May 4, 1976, EFG 1977, 64, had to deal with a trust which comprised a limited partnership interest in a German limited partnership, and it treated the income attributed to the Geman-resident beneficiary as business income; this case implies that the flow of income through a trust does not change its character. Furthermore the Tax Court Baden-Württemberg held on December 12, 1979, EFG 1980, 346, that the interest and dividend income collected by an executor under New York law (no trust apparently was involved) could not be attributed to the German-resident beneficiary as long as the income was not actually distributed to the beneficiary and as long as the beneficiary had no claim of right to receive such income currently. In the reasons of the decision, the tax court expressly referred to corresponding inheritance tax decisions concerning testamentary trusts, and the tax court decision was affirmed on appeal by the BFH on May 29, 1984, RIW 1984, 923, even though the BFH indicated that it might have favoured another decision. Nevertheless, this decision might imply also that income derived by a trust does not change its character as a dividend or as interest even though the incidence of taxation may be deferred until actual distribution.

5. Similar considerations apply so far as the wealth tax *(Vermögenssteuer)* status of German-resident creators or beneficiaries is concerned.

Problem 1

1. All of the income of the trust and irrespective of whether it is currently distributed or retained presumably would be taxed to the beneficiary if the trust were to be considered the equivalent of a family foundation under Section 15 AStG. Nevertheless, no clear-cut case law has been reported so far. Four recent articles in legal periodicals have taken the position that an irrevocable trust cannot be viewed as the equivalent of a family foundation or some other unincorporated entity but such articles do not bind the administration or the courts. See Pöllath, IWB 3 Deutschland Gruppe 1, p. 1079, at p. 1084; Ratjen, DB 1982, 1793; Peiner, RIW 1983, 593; Otto, RIW 1982, 491. The decision of the Tax Court Baden-Württemberg of December 12, 1979, and the decision of the BFH on appeal of May 29, 1984 (see under no. 4 of the introductory remarks) presumably would suggest a deferment of the incidence of the German income tax until actual distribution of the income.

2(i). If the income is currently distributed, then we believe that the beneficiary may be taxable. In this case, the income could either be treated as other periodical income under Section 22(1) EStG or the trust could be considered a mere conduit under general principles of German tax law or under Section 15 AStG in which case the character of the income would remain unchanged. It is believed that the latter treatment should be more appropriate.

2(ii). We believe that under the decision of the Tax Court Baden-Würtemberg of December 12, 1979, the taxation would be deferred until actual distribution unless Section 15 AStG (family foundation) should be applicable.

2(iii). In this case, we believe that the income actually distributed would be taxable to the beneficiary whereas the undistributed portion might not be taxed until actual distribution occurs.

3. It may be either treated as other periodical income or it may retain the character of the underlying income derived by the trust depending on which theory ultimately will be adopted by the courts.

Problem 2

1(a). The residence of the creator of the trust can expose the trust to German income taxation as a resident taxpayer if the trust is viewed as the equivalent of a family foundation or another incorporated entity and if the creator actually manages the investments of the trust. Nevertheless, since the creator has no power over the trust's assets or its administration, these requirements clearly are not met. Furthermore, if the income of the trust is currently attributable to the creator under Section 15 AStG, the trust will not qualify as a taxable entity in the first place. Section 3(1) KStG.

1(b). If the trust had been created under German law and if it were viewed as a family foundation or another unincorporated entity then it would have its registered seat in Germany and, therefore, would qualify as a German resident under Section 1 KStG. Nevertheless, this question is moot as German civil law does not permit the creation of a common law trust.

1(c). If the trust were considered the equivalent of a family foundation or another unincorporated entity, then the trustee could constitute the principal place of management of the trust. In this case the trust would be considered a German resident for German income tax purposes.

1(d). Even if the trust should be considered as the equivalent of a family foundation or another unincorporated entity, it could not be considered a German resident merely because the beneficiary is a resident of Germany, in particular since the beneficiary has no power over the trust's assets or its administration.

2(i). No, the residence of the trust (if it can be considered a family foundation or another unincorporated entity) is determined irrespective of whether the trust distributes its income currently or not.

2(ii). See at *2(i),* above.

2(iii). See at *2(i),* above.

Problem 3

1(a). German tax treaties invariably require the German payor of a dividend to apply a withholding tax at the regular rate of 25% subject to a claim for refund which has to be filed by or on behalf of the recipient of the dividend. The German tax administration does not recognize a mere fiduciary *(Treuhänder)* as entitled to a refund under a treaty; instead, the application has to be filed by or on behalf of the grantor, or beneficiary. See, e.g., the dividend withholding tax refund form under the US-German Tax Treaty footnote 1; see also Annotation 118 through 120 to Art. II of the US-German Tax Treaty in Debatin/Walter, Handbook on the United States – German Tax Convention.

1(b). German withholding taxes are payable when the dividend is paid by the distributing corporation irrespective of whether an intermediary retains the dividend or redistributes it to a beneficiary.

1(c). See at *1(b),* above.

2(a). German withholding tax is imposed at the time when the dividend is received by the recipient and this applies irrespective of whether the recipient is deemed to be the trustee or beneficiary. However, so far as the refund claim is concerned the proper party to file such a claim most likely would be the beneficiary and it would certainly be easier to establish his standing if he could show that the trust currently distributed the German source dividends to him. Nevertheless, in our view the distribution pattern should not be decisive

2(b). See at *2(a)*, above.

2(c). See at *2(a)*, above.

3(a). The answer should be the same as in *2(a)*, above.

3(b). See at *2(a)*, above.

Problem 4

1. If the trust is considered the equivalent of a foreign family foundation, then not only the income of the trust is attributed to the beneficiary but such income retains its characteristics and source. Runge, DB 1977, 514 at 516; Baranowski, *Besteuerung von Auslandsbeziehungen*, 1978, p. 299; cf. Flick/Wassermeyer/Becker, ibid, annotations 22 *et seq*. to Section 15 AStG. This means, that the country A withholding tax will be deemed paid for the account of the beneficiary and available to him for German foreign tax credit purposes. These rules apply irrespective of whether the trust distributes part or all of the dividends to the beneficiary.

2. If the trust is deemed to constitute a mere conduit or the equivalent of a foreign family foundation, then the dividend income will be deemed to be derived from sources within country A. See at 1, above. Alternatively, if the trust should be considered some kind of other unincorporated entity which collects the dividend in its own name and for its own account, then distributions by the trust could be deemed to be derived from sources within country B.

3. If the trust is deemed to constitute the equivalent of a foreign family foundation under Section 15 AstG, then the country B tax is creditable against German income taxes under Section 15(5) AStG which refers to sections 12, 10(1) AstG. In all other instances, Country B tax most likely will not be eligible as a credit against the Country C tax.

Problem 5

1. If and so long as the creator of the trust has the power to revoke the trust and to repossess its assets, such assets as well as the income derived therefrom will be attributed to the creator and the trust will be disregarded. Section 39(1)(2) AO; for further reference see paragraph 1 of the introductory remarks. The result of this current attribution of all the assets and the income to the creator is as follows:

(a) In the set of facts described in Problem 1, the beneficiary would not be taxable on any portion of the income derived by the trust; the actual distribution of income by the trust to the beneficiary presumably would constitute a gift by the creator to the beneficiary which may attract a gift tax.

(b) Under the circumstances presented in Problem 2, the trust would be disregarded for German tax purposes and, therefore, would not be considered a resident for German income tax purposes irrespective of whether Germany were country A, country B, country C or country D. The answer does not depend on whether, by the terms of the trust instrument, the income of the trust is distributable or not.

(c) So far as Problem 3 is concerned, creator is a resident of country B and, for this reason, Germany would have to accept a claim for refund by the creator under the income tax treaty between Germany and country B. Conversely, if there was no tax treaty between Germany and country B but a treaty between Germany and country C, no refund claim would be available.

(d) Under the set of facts described in Problem 4, country A withholding tax will be deemed to have been paid for the account of the creator if Germany is country B. Also it will be deemed to be received from sources within country A for German foreign tax credit rules. If Germany were country C, the issue would be moot as the income of the revocable trust will be attributed to the creator and not to the beneficiary.

2. There are no authorities in point. Nevertheless for sucession law purposes, the existence of a general power of appointment in favour of a life beneficiary has been interpreted to mean that the beneficiary obtained full control of the assets and, therefore, should be treated as the full and unrestricted heir of the decedent. See Ferid/Firsching, *Internationales Erbrecht,* US Grdz. C III, annotation 62(g).

On this basis, we believe that if the beneficiary were given the power to require the trust assets to be transferred to him in whole or in part at any time, the assets and the income derived therefrom should be currently attributed to the beneficiary under Section 39(1)(2) AO. As a result, the responses given in 1, above, would change in that the beneficiary would take the place of the creator.

Bibliography – Germany

A) *Income Tax*

I. *Court Decisions*

(1) *Bundesfinanzhof*

(a) BFH decision of July 20, 1971, BStBl. 1972 II 170
(b) BFH decision of May 29, 1984, RIW 1984, 923: DB 1984, 2175

(2) *Tax Courts*

(a) Tax Court Hannover of October 23, 1964, EFG 1965, 225
(b) Tax Court Berlin of May 4, 1976, EFG 1977, 64
(c) Tax Court Baden-Württemberg of December 12, 1979, EFG 1980, 346

II. *Administrative rulings*

1. Finance Ministry Nordrhein-Westfalen of February 16, 1968, DB 1968, 330
2. Finance Ministry Niedersachsen of March 19, 1968, EStKP 2 EStG Nr. 1

III. *Other authorities*

1. J. C. Killius, German Inheritance and Income Taxation of U.S. estates, 24 *Tax Law Review* (1968) 127, at pp. 150 *et seq*.
2. M. Ratjen, *Der US-amerikanische Discretionary trust im deutschen Steuerrecht*, DB 1982, 1973, at 1795.

B. *Wealth Tax*

I. *Court Decisions*

1. *Reichsfinanzhof/Bundesfinanzhof*

(a) RFH decision of October 14, 1937, RStBl. 1938, 10;
(b) RFH decision of January 11, 1940, RStBl. 1940, 267;
(c) BFH decision of August 4, 1961, HFR 1962, 52.
(d) BFH decision of May 7, 1986, BStBl. 1986 II 615.

2. *Tax Courts*

(a) Tax Court Hamburg of August 9, 1979, EFG 1980, 81 (decision on appeal see at I 1 (d), above.)
(b) Tax Court Kassel of April 8, 1981, EFG 1981, 439.
(c) Tax Court Baden-Württemberg of September 15, 1982, EFG 1983, 260

II. *Administrative Rulings*

OFD Frankfurt of October 4, 1982, NWB F 1 S. 333.

III. *Other authorities*

M. Ratjen, ibid., at 1796.

SWITZERLAND

Mr. Pierre Gillioz

I. Introductory remarks

The concept of trust does not exist under Swiss civil law and no specific tax provision governing trusts is to be found in the federal and cantonal income and net worth tax laws.

From a civil law standpoint, the Swiss Federal Tribunal has confirmed that an Anglo-American trust could not be assimilated to any existing Swiss institution. Having to apply Swiss law for specific reasons of the case under review, our Supreme Court held that an Anglo-American trust was to be qualified, under Swiss law, as an *agreement* containing elements from various Swiss institutions such as the agency agreement, the fiduciary transfer of ownership, the donation and the contract in favour of a third party (*'stipulation pour autrui'*) (see *Harrison* v *Crédit Suisse*, RO 96 II 79).

In the absence of any specific tax provision governing trusts, Swiss tax authorities and Swiss tax jurisdictions take a similar approach to that of the civil law courts. They basically try and qualify the trust under review by comparison with the most similar institutions existing under Swiss law.

As a rule, trusts (except for Charitable trusts) are not considered to be foundations. Trustees are regarded as fiduciary owners and beneficiaries are treated as the real owners of the income derived from and of the property held on trust. Tenants for life are normally assimilated to beneficiaries of a usufruct whereas remaindermen are treated as formal owners.

Trusts are, therefore, not treated as a separate taxpayer and are not subject to tax *per se*. Trustees are exempt from tax as are nominee owners under Swiss tax laws. Beneficiaries are taxed according to their rights in the trust.

However, one should keep in mind that very few cases of trusts have been tried by courts. In addition, Swiss tax authorities are somewhat reluctant to give information on the tax treatment of trusts, either because they lack experience in that area, or because they feel that, by reason of their diversity, trusts are to be treated on a case basis along the general principles briefly described above.

Therefore, it has not always been possible to answer very precisely the problems raised in this publication and uncertainties remain in many areas in the absence of any tax law provision, case law and well established administrative practice.

Problem 1

(a) The terms of the trust settlement are, for the reasons mentioned in the introductory remarks, of the utmost importance. If one assumes that the trust under review has been set up irrevocably and that the beneficiary is clearly designated and can not be changed, even by the trustees, then Swiss tax authorities will consider that the beneficiary is the sole owner of the trust's assets and of its income.

(b) If all of the trust income is distributed currently, the beneficiary will clearly be subject to income tax in Switzerland. He will also be subject to net worth taxes if he is the sole beneficiary even though he will only be entitled to the capital of thc trust later on.

If the income is accumulated or only partly distributed the question is more complex. Indeed, individuals are taxable, in Switzerland, on a cash basis. Therefore, a beneficiary should not be subject to tax until he has actually received the trust's income. On the other hand, one should not ignore that the existence of trusts is basically disregarded by the Swiss tax authorities. They could, therefore, take the position that any income generated by the trust's assets are to be considered as income earned by the beneficiary, whether actually distributed or not.

In the event that the income has not been effectively distributed but the beneficiary has the right to require its payment, then it is likely that income will be immediately taxable on the beneficiary.

(c) As a rule, since beneficiaries are deemed to be the sole owners of the trust's assets and of its income, it is the underlying income derived by the trust which is taken into account for Swiss income tax purposes. One should note, in that context, that any income derived by an individual resident of Switzerland is basically subject to income taxes, whatever its source. However, capital gains realised by individuals, which do not arise from their business activities, are fully exempt from income tax.

Problem 2

(a) Since the trust is, as a rule, not considered to be a separate taxpayer, the question of residence is not necessarily relevant for income and net worth tax purposes in Switzerland.

If one assumes that the trust was set up irrevocably for the benefit of a sole beneficiary which may not be changed, Switzerland will tax the trust's assets and the trust's income only in the event that the beneficiary is resident in our country.

In particular, the mere fact that a trustee is resident in Switzerland does not entail income and net worth taxation, because the trustee is considered to be in the position of a nominee owner, not subject to tax. For the same reasons, the domicile of the creator and the laws of incorporation of the trust are not relevant for internal tax purposes. One should point out, however, that the domicile of the creator may be important for gift and inheritance tax purposes and that the residence of the trust may be taken into account for tax treaty purposes.

(b) With respect to residence problems, the mere fact that income is distributed currently or is accumulated until a future date or is partly distributed and partly accumulated has no impact on the residence question. As already pointed out, however, the time of distribution may be important for determining when the income is effectively taxed in the hands of the beneficiary.

Problem 3

Generally speaking, a trust is not considered to be a resident for tax treaty purposes and therefore not entitled to claim treaty benefits. An exception is made to this rule whenever a trust is treated as a separate taxpayer and is effectively taxed in a tax treaty country. As a result, whenever a trust is involved in the application of a tax treaty, Swiss authorities require from the trustee that he disclose the name and the place of residence of the beneficiaries and apply to the payment made to the trust the provisions of the double tax treaty existing between Switzerland and the country of residence of the beneficiary. If, however, the trustee can demonstrate that under the law of its residence, the trust is considered to be a separate taxpayer fully subject to tax, then Swiss authorities are also prepared to apply the provisions of the tax treaty existing between Switzerland and the country of residence of the trust.

Problem 4

In Switzerland, foreign tax credit is available only under certain double tax treaties. Therefore, the beneficiary which is a resident of Switzerland will be entitled to a foreign tax credit if our country is bound by a double tax treaty providing for such a credit with the country of source of the income.

Swiss tax authorities normally disregard the existence of trust and therefore normally refuse to apply the tax treaty which may exist between the country where the beneficiary is resident and the country where the trust is resident. As mentioned above, however, an exception is made whenever the trust is effectively subject to tax in the country where it is a resident and is entitled to the benefit of the tax treaties.

Problem 5

(a) As a rule, Swiss tax authorities consider that no transfer of ownership has taken place as long as the trust is revocable. In such a case, therefore, the creator is deemed to be the sole owner of the trust's assets and the sole beneficiary of its income. If domiciled in Switzerland the creator will be subject to income and net worth taxes on all the trust's assets and trust's income.

(b) If a beneficiary is only entitled to the income and has no power to require the trust's assets to be transferred to him in whole or in part, he will be taxable on the income of the trust but not on its capital. If such beneficiary is entitled to require the transfer of the trust's assets in his favour then he will be also subject to net worth taxes on the trust's assets, whether or not he requires such transfer.

II. Conclusions

An interesting case was brought before the Swiss Supreme Court. It can be briefly summarized as follows:

Under a trust set up in a common law country, a beneficiary domiciled in Switzerland was entitled to the income of the trust whereas remaindermen domiciled in another country than Switzerland were entitled, upon the death of the tenant for life, to the capital of the trust. The trust's assets essentially consisted of stock in various corporations. At a certain time, one of the companies in which the trust had an interest made a distribution of stock instead of a distribution of dividends.

The question arose whether such distribution of stock was taxable in the hands of the beneficiary domiciled in Switzerland. Indeed, individuals resident in Switzerland are subject to income tax distributions of stock as they are on distribution of dividends in cash, even if they only have a usufruct on the stock and are not full owner of such stock.

The Swiss tax authorities wanted to tax this distribution of stock on the beneficiary domiciled in Switzerland, whereas the taxpayer argued that the stock received belonged to the trust's assets on which he had no right.

The Swiss Federal Tribunal considered that such a distribution of stock was not taxable on the beneficiary domiciled in Switzerland because he was entitled only to the income of the trust and not to the assets which were transferred to the trust. Since, in the instant case, the tenant for life would never receive the stock distributed to the trust, he was held not to be subject to tax thereon. (see RO 85 I 115)

This decision is a good illustration of the approach of the Swiss tax courts when dealing with trusts. Indeed, although they tend to tax beneficiaries like taxpayers who are entitled to similar rights under Swiss law institutions, they nonetheless do take into account the peculiarities of Anglo-American trusts. In the instant case, the fact that the situation of a beneficiary, under a trust, was not totally similar to that of a usufructuary was considered important enough to treat him differently.

UNITED STATES

Prof. Harvey Dale

Introductory Remarks

The common law trust is a widely recognized concept in the United States. Subject to the exceptions discussed below, under Section 641 of the United States Internal Revenue Code of 1986 [1] (the 'IRC'), a trust is treated as a separate taxpayer and is taxable at the rates of tax which apply to individual taxpayers. As such, trusts must declare their own income, deductions, credits and exemptions. Exceptions to this rule, as well as the ultimate tax consequences to the beneficiary and the creator of the trust, depend primarily on the particular terms of the trust.

To the extent that the creator (or a beneficiary) possesses certain specified powers, such as the power to revoke the trust or to transfer the trust assets to himself, the general rules do not apply and the trust normally is not treated as a separate taxable entity. If the creator retains any of the powers set forth in IRC Sections 673–677, the trust will be deemed a 'grantor trust'. Under IRC Section 676, for example, the income of a grantor trust would be taxable to the creator, and the trust would not be treated as a separate taxpayer, where the creator is given the power to revoke the trust. Similarly, to the extent that the beneficiary has the capacity, under the terms of the trust, to vest the trust corpus in himself, under IRC Section 678 the beneficiary is treated as the owner of the trust and the trust generally is not treated as a separate taxable entity.

In the more commonplace case of a 'non-grantor' trust, however, in which the creator and the beneficiary do not have such powers, the trust will be treated as a separate taxpayer. In such cases, the beneficiary generally will be taxable on all trust income to the extent that the trust instrument requires that such income be distributed currently, whether or not such income is, in fact, distributed currently to the beneficiary (and as long as the trust does not provide for the payment or reserving of trust funds for charitable purposes). To the extent that the trust

1. Except where noted, most provisions of the IRC relating to the taxation of trusts were not changed by the Tax Reform Act of 1986 and were carried over from the United States Internal Revenue Code of 1954, as amended.

instrument requires or permits income to be accumulated, the beneficiary generally will be taxable only upon actual distributions of the income; however, once distributed to the beneficiary, accumulated income will be treated as having been distributed in previous years under IRC Sections 665–668 (the 'throwback' rules).

The following problem sets demonstrate how some of these basic principles of trust taxation apply in a transnational context where the creator, trust, trustee, beneficiary and income do not all come from the same jurisdiction.

Problem 1 – Entity Characterization

(1) As indicated in the introductory remarks, the trust would be treated as a separate taxpayer; however, the tax treatment of the beneficiary depends upon the terms of the trust and the additional factors described below.

(i) If the terms of the trust provide that all of its income is required to be distributed currently (and do not provide for the payment or setting aside of funds for charitable purposes), the amount of income required to be distributed currently would be taxable to the beneficiary under IRC Section 652 whether or not such income is actually distributed.

(ii) Conversely, if the terms of the trust require accumulation of trust income until some future time, the beneficiary would not be taxable until such future time. However, once remitted to the beneficiary, the income of the trust would be treated as having been distributed in earlier years under the 'throwback' rules of IRC Sections 665–668. Thus, in the case of a U.S. trust which distributes accumulated income to a U.S. person, the accumulation distribution is deemed to have been distributed on the last day of the earliest preceding taxable year with undistributed net income. Additionally, the amount of U.S. taxes imposed on a trust for the throwback year, attributable to the accumulation distribution, is deemed an additional distribution to the beneficiary. The beneficiary then must compute the amount of tax owed on the grossed-up distribution (a computation for which special rules are provided), credit against the tax due the taxes previously paid by the trust and included in his income as an additional deemed distribution, and pay the net tax due. Accumulation distributions from a foreign trust to U.S. persons are taxed in the manner described above, and, in addition, a non-deductible 6% interest charge is also imposed on the amount of taxes due.

(iii) If the terms of the trust give the trustee discretion either to distribute or accumulate trust income, the beneficiary would be taxable under IRC Section 662 when and to the extent that the trust income is in fact distributed. Amounts distributed in any taxable year in excess of the trust's 'distributable net income', as such term is defined in IRC Section 662, for such year would be subject to the throwback rules noted above.

(iv) In most cases, income derived by a trust which is passed through currently to the beneficiary retains the same character in the hands of the beneficiary as it had in the hands of the trust according to IRC Sections 652 and 662. This can be an advantage or a disadvantage, depending upon the particular facts. For example, in *Maximov v. United States*, 373 U.S. 49 (1963), a U.S. trust realized capital gains income for the two years in question; however, the gains were added to the trust corpus and not distributed to the nonresident alien beneficiaries in the years in which the gains were realized. The trust was held to be taxable on the gains even though, had such amounts been distributed currently to the nonresident alien beneficiaries, the beneficiaries would have been deemed to have received a capital gain exempt from U.S. taxation under the U.S. – U.K. Tax Treaty.

Under IRC Section 667, income which is distributed to the beneficiary in a year subsequent to when it was derived by the trust retains its character only to the extent that such income is distributed to a nonresident alien individual (or foreign corporation), that it consists of tax exempt interest income (IRC Section 103), or that it is necessary to apply certain foreign tax credit limitations; otherwise the income is treated as undifferentiated ordinary income.

Problem 2 – Residence Criteria

(1) There is no single meaningful statutory definition of resident and nonresident trusts for U.S. federal income tax purposes. (The rules of IRC Section 7701(b), including the 'substantial presence' test, do not apply to trusts). IRC Section 7701(a) (31) defines a 'foreign trust' as a trust, the income of which from sources outside the United States and which is not effectively connected with a trade or business in the United States, is not includible in gross income. However, this is really a conclusion, rather than a definition. Various rulings and cases in this area have established that the trust's residence is determined by several factors, which include the situs of the trust's creation, its place of administration, the trustee's primary residence, and the Creator's residence.

(a) If the trust's only connection with the United States were the Creator's U.S. residence, the United States would probably not view the trust as a U.S. resident. The IRC Section 679 provisions dealing with 'foreign trusts' having U.S. beneficiaries contemplate that a U.S. person may be the creator of a 'foreign' trust. The Creator's U.S. residence might be one factor that, in combination with other factors, would tend to cause the characterization of the trust as a U.S. resident; however, taken alone, this factor would be insufficient to give the trust U.S. residence.

(b) If the trust's only connection with the United States were the mere fact that the trust was formed pursuant to the laws of the United States, this factor alone presumably would not be sufficient to cause the trust to be characterized as a U.S. resident, even though it would help to establish U.S. residence in conjunction with additional U.S. contacts. Because it is not possible for a *citizen* of the United States to be classified as a non-resident *alien,* it is conceivable that the 'alienage', i.e., residence, of a trust created under U.S. law would be viewed as a foregone conclusion, although no authority expressly so indicates. In Rev. Rul. 60–181, 1960–1 C.B. 257 it was held that a trust established under the laws of a foreign jurisdiction but consisting of U.S. property and administered by a U.S. trustee, was a U.S. resident for purposes of U.S. Federal Income Taxation; therefore, if it is not the United States, the governing law of the trust cannot be viewed as the single determining factor of the residence of a trust.

(c) The U.S. residence of the trustee is a highly pertinent factor that would be given much weight. In *B.W. Jones Trust,* 46 B.T.A. 531, *aff'd,* 132 F.2d 914 (4th Cir. 1943), trusts created under the laws of the United Kingdom were deemed U.S. residents because of the fact that they were administered by a U.S. trustee and because the trust consisted of U.S. assets. The residence of the trustee is considered to be a highly significant variable and, therefore, it is possible that this factor alone could be sufficient to establish U.S. residence, although there is no authority directly on point.

(d) Standing alone, the beneficiary's U.S. residence would not cause the trust itself to be characterized as a U.S. resident. Several statutory provisions *(e.g.,* IRC Section 668) which deal with the taxation of U.S. beneficiaries of 'foreign' trusts, clearly contemplate that U.S. persons may be the beneficiaries of 'foreign' trusts.

(2) The actual terms of the trust regarding distributions do not directly effect the residence of the trust. However, to the extent that the trust

requires income to be accumulated, the terms of the trust may be more relevant to the residence of the trust because (as will be explained below) then the place of administration becomes more important.

(i) If the terms of the trust require the income to be distributed currently, the terms of the trust should have no bearing on the trust's residence.

(ii) To the extent that the terms of the trust require the income to be accumulated until some future time, the residence of the trust could be affected indirectly by this factor, in that the place of administration of the trust, which would include the administration of its accumulated income, arguably would be a more significant factor in determining the trust's residence.

(iii) As the answers to questions (2) (i) & (ii) indicate, to the extent that income is required to be distributed currently, the residence of the trust is less affected by the terms of the trust; conversely, to the extent that income is accumulated, the residence of the trust is indirectly affected by the trust's terms.

Problem 3

If country A were the United States, the trust (which is created and administered in country B) would be treated for tax purposes as if it were a nonresident alien individual. The trust's income would be computed in the same manner as the gross income of an individual for the reasons set forth in problem 1, and the trust would be treated as a nonresident alien because the facts set forth in this problem would clearly not render the trust a resident of country A. *See* Rev. Rul. 68–621, 1968–2 C.B. 286, which holds that a nonresident alien estate is taxed on income received from sources within the United States including capital gains and dividends received; however, the estate is allowed deductions for distributions not in excess of 'distributable net income' and the administrator must withhold U.S. taxes from the dividend distributions.

(1) (a) The dividend distributed from country A to the trust in country B would, at the first level, be subject to a withholding tax at the reduced rate of 15%, because of the treaty between country A and country B, regardless of the residence of the beneficiary. However, at the second level, under IRC Section 662, the beneficiary would be required to include in his taxable income the amounts distributed to him by the

trust, and such income would be considered to have the same character in the hands of the beneficiary as it had in the hands of the trust. Accordingly, the beneficiary would be subject to the 25% (withholding) tax rate because there is no tax treaty between country B and country C, and the 15% tax withheld initially upon the payment to the trust would be deemed to have been paid by the beneficiary under Reg. Section 1.1462–1(b), which states that taxes withheld at the source on income paid to a fiduciary are deemed to have been paid by the taxpayer ultimately liable for the tax upon the income. The trust, making current distributions to the beneficiary, would be obligated under Reg. Section 1.1441–3(f) (which requires domestic fiduciaries to withhold the tax at the source on certain items which constitute gross income from U.S. sources of beneficiaries who are non-U.S. persons) to withhold the additional 10% tax when remitting the income to the beneficiary.

(b) In the case of a trust which accumulates income the same general principles would apply, as to the tax rates applicable to the trust and to the beneficiary. However, in this case, the beneficiary would be taxed only in accordance with the throwback rules of IRC Sections 665–668, which would treat the income as having been distributed in earlier years.

(c) Again the same principles set forth in 1(a) would apply as to the rate of taxation at the trust level and at the beneficiary level.

(2)(a) In the case where there is no tax treaty between country A and country B, dividends distributed from country A to the trust in country B would be subject to the 25% rate of withholding at the initial trust level. However, because the treaty between country B and country C would entitle the beneficiary to be taxed at the reduced withholding rate of 15%, the beneficiary should be able to claim a refund for the excess withholding tax paid to the trust (10%) under Reg. Section 301.6402–3(e). Such regulation requires nonresident aliens and foreign corporations to file for a refund by showing the taxpayer's entire income subject to the tax with a statement claiming a refund by the taxpayer, as beneficial owner. Query the effect of IRC Section 6401(b)(2), which limits the availability of credits for such overwithheld taxes to cases in which nonresident aliens qualify for and make certain elections to be treated as residents of the United States.

(b)&(c) If the trust were to accumulate income, the same principles set forth in 2(a) would apply as to the rate of taxation at the trust and at the beneficiary level. Thus, under Reg. Section 1.1462–1(b) (see Problem 1(a)) the 25% tax, which would continue to be withheld initially

upon the payment to the trust, would be deemed to have been paid by the beneficiary, and the excess withholding tax would have to be recovered through a refund claim. *But see* IRC Section 6401(b)(2). Furthermore, the beneficiary would be taxed in accordance with the distribution rules set forth in Problem 1.

(3)(a)&(b) As question (2) indicates, the beneficiary may claim a 10% refund if the 25% withholding tax is imposed by country A at the point when the beneficiary is taxed.

Problem 4 – Source of Trust Distributions – indirect tax credits

(1) If country C, the residence of the beneficiary, were the United States, and a country A withholding tax on the income were paid by the trust, the beneficiary would be entitled to claim a foreign tax credit for his 'proportionate share' of taxes paid or accrued by the trust under Section 901(b)(5) which specifically allows beneficiaries of a trust to claim a tax credit for their proportionate share of taxes paid by the trust to a foreign country. There is some uncertainty about the details of the beneficiary's foreign tax credit calculations, however.

(2) Under IRC 667(e), the source of income would be considered to be country A. The source of the income could be relevant.

(3) If a tax is imposed on the trust by country B, the beneficiary would be able to claim a foreign tax credit under IRC Section 901(b) (5). The U.S. foreign tax credit limitation is presently computed on an over-all basis, rather than on a per country basis. If as under prior law a per country limitation were applicable, there would be no country B income with which to absorb the foreign tax credit.

Problem 5 – Grantor Trusts

(1) The power of the creator to revoke the trust and repossess its assets would result in substantial revisions to the tax consequences described above. Under IRC Section 676, the power to revoke the trust would cause the trust to be characterized as a so-called grantor trust. As a general rule, a grantor trust is not treated as a separate entity for federal income tax purposes; instead, the existence of such a trust is largely ignored and the income, deductions, etc., of the trust are taxable to the grantor. A grantor trust created by a nonresident alien for the benefit of a U.S. beneficiary therefore permits the beneficiary to receive trust income, as a gift, free of all U.S. income taxation, (provided such

income is not subject to U.S. taxation in the hands of the grantor). In Rev. Rul. 69–70, 1969–1 C.B. 182, the creator (a nonresident alien) of a foreign trust was treated as the owner of such trust, and therefore the U.S. beneficiary of the trust was not taxable on distributions of the trust deemed to be owned by the grantor. The other circumstances in which a grantor is treated as the owner of all or a portion of a trust have been expanded in the Tax Reform Act of 1986 and are specified in IRC Sections 673–675 and 677. In addition, IRC Section 679 indicates that a United States person who directly or indirectly transfers property to a foreign trust having one or more U.S. beneficiaries is treated as the owner of the portion of the trust attributable to such property.

(2) The power of the beneficiary to require the trust assets to be transferred to himself in whole or in part would have parallel implications. Under IRC Section 678, a person other than the Creator of the trust who has a power to vest in himself the corpus or the income of a trust (which is not otherwise a grantor trust) is treated as the grantor of such trust.

II. SUMMARY OF THE PROCEEDINGS

Dr. J Barry Bracewell-Milnes

Professor Harvey P. Dale, United States, Chairman of the Seminar, introduced the Panelists who were:- Mr. Pierre Gillioz, Switzerland; Dr. Jürgen Killius, Germany; Mr. John King, Australia; Mr. F. Tripet, France; and Professor Donald Trautman, United States. He referred to the written materials which had been distributed to those present, consisting of an outline of the Seminar, a set of five problems, material on the five countries and an article on the Hague Convention on Trusts. The terms 'trust', 'trustee', 'grantor' and 'beneficiary' would be used only in English and not translated. The Seminar was about personal trusts and would not be concerned with business, charitable, protective or investment trusts. Three types of common law trusts would be under discussion – revocable trusts (which were ignored for tax purposes), simple trusts (requiring the immediate distribution of income) and accumulating trusts. The Seminar was confined to the taxation of income, and within this area it was accumulating trusts which posed the most interesting problems. The Seminar would be concerned with common law trusts in both common law and civil law jurisdictions; but it would not be concerned with other forms of fiduciary arrangement. He concluded by explaining the scheme of proceedings for the afternoon. First, Professor Trautman would speak about the general nature of a common law trust; he would not be discussing the taxation of trusts. Then the speakers from the five countries would give a brief overview of the tax treatment of trusts in each country. Finally, the Panel would discuss the problems set out in the materials already distributed.

Professor Trautman

Professor Trautman said that he would not be speaking about the tax aspects of the subject, but concentrating on the aspects of trusts which were difficult for civil law countries. Trusts had begun as an evasionary device – a device for evading a wide range of legal obligations which would have been incurred if the property concerned had been held absolutely. Trusts had first been used to shift title without the undesireable consequences that might have been incurred if the title had been shifted in other ways. But trusts had merits going beyond these evasionary purposes. For the purposes of the family law, trusts could secure the rational and controlled passage of title to future generations through the nomination of a manager to manage family funds. For business purposes, a trust could be more effective than either an agency or a corporation for looking after the interests of investors, especially if the beneficiaries were not those who had originally made the investment. A trust was not a contractual arrangement, but an arrangement for the passage of title. Enjoyment was sharply distinguished from legal title; the beneficiaries had equitable title to the trust funds, but not legal title. Except in a revocable trust, the duties of the trustees were owed to the beneficiaries and not to the grantor or the settlor. The terms of the trust could take account of the settlor's wishes, subject to mandatory provisions of law; but enforcement of the terms of the trust was in the hands of the beneficiaries. This posed particular problems for charitable trusts where there were no identifiable beneficiaries; here the rights of enforcement were in the hands of the Attorney General. The obligation of the trustee was to act in accordance with the terms of the trust; provided that he did so, he could act independently of the wishes of the beneficiaries, or even in conflict with those wishes.

A trust was not a legal entity. There were many similarities between a trust and an agency arrangement or a corporation. There were also similarities with civil law concepts, such as executorship, guardianship and *Treuhand*. However, these concepts, although they did similar work in civil law countries to the work done by trusts in common law countries, were more discreet and limited in scope.

Trusts were used by analogy to solve otherwise insoluble problems. Large charities could be set up either as trusts or corporations, often without much tax consequence either way. Among personal trusts the main distinctions were between revocable and irrevocable trusts; between testamentary and *inter vivos* trusts; and between discretionary trusts with settled interests in possession.

Professor Trautman concluded his address with a discussion of the International Convention on the Recognition of trusts (the Hague Convention). It was important to emphasise that under Article 19 the Convention had no effect for fiscal purposes. The purpose of the Convention was partly educational: it was intended to familiarise people brought up in the civil law tradition with the concept of trusts, and in this connection the Convention served as a model for judicial decisions. The subject of the Convention was the treatment in civil law countries of trusts established in common law countries. The Convention was not intended to introduce trusts into the domestic law of civil law countries (although this was happening gradually anyway). The Convention also sought to prevent the use of trusts for purposes which conflicted with settled policy in the signatory countries. Article 4 said that the Convention was limited to trust problems and did not extend to preliminary issues (such as the validity of a will or deed, the rule against perpetuities, and so on). Article 14 said that countries might go beyond the Convention in recognising the institution of the trust. The choice-of-law rules were similar to the rules for contracts. The settlor was free to choose the law governing the trust, subject to conditions. Any trust which complied with the rules for applicable law must be recognised. So far, Italy, the Netherlands and the United Kingdom had signed the Convention, but none had ratified.

Country Interviews

Professor Dale introduced a discussion of each country's tax treatment of common law trusts, beginning with the common law countries.

Mr. King said that Australia was a common law country. The law of trusts in Australia was based on English law, although the income tax law was quite different. As in England, most trusts had originally been family settlements or trusts for charitable purposes. The avoidance of estate and death taxes had come to be an important consideration. In the last ten to fifteen years trusts had increasingly come to be used as a form of business organisation, including investment trusts on the lines of a mutual fund. As in the United Kingdom and the United States, a trust was not a legal entity in Australia; but it had to file an income tax return as though it were a taxpayer. The general principle governing the liability of trusts to income tax was a see-through rule: it was the beneficiaries who were taxable. The actual time of the distribution of trust income was irrelevant; the decisive criterion was the entitlement of beneficiaries at the end of the tax year. The trustee was taxable on the residual income of the trust – where no beneficiary was entitled to the income or where it was impossible to say which beneficiary was so entitled. If income was taxed in the hands of the trustee, it was not taxed on distribution to the beneficiaries as well. The exception to all this was that in grantor trusts the settlor was taxable on the whole of the trust income.

Professor Dale said that in the United States trusts were regarded as a normal planning vehicle. Since the early 1980s about one and a half million trusts had prepared and filed income tax returns each year. In grantor trusts, where the settlor retained powers over the trust, the income of the trust was taxable as the income of the grantor and the expenses of the trust were similarly deductible. Foreign trusts established by a US person for the benefit of a US person were treated as grantor trusts. Spouse-interest trusts were also treated as grantor trusts. If the income of a grantor trust was distributed to someone other than the grantor, it was not taxed again but treated as a gift. Simple trusts were regarded as conduits between the income and the beneficiaries. A simple trust computed its distributable net income (DNI) and reported it to the tax authorities; but tax was charged and paid at the level of the beneficiaries. In accumulation trusts distributed income was taxed as for simple trusts; but accumulation trusts were themselves taxable on undistributed DNI. On a subsequent distribution of income already taxed at the level of the trust, the income was taxable a second time in the hands of the beneficiary; but for these 'throwback' distributions the beneficiary was entitled to a credit for the tax previously paid at the level of the trust. If this credit was inadequate to cover the beneficiary's tax liability, no interest charge was levied on the element of 'deferral' inherent in the difference; but, if the beneficiary's liability was less than the tax already levied on the trust, the difference was not refunded. On throwback distributions from foreign trusts, by contrast with domestic trusts, an interest charge was levied if the tax liability of the beneficiary exceeded the tax already paid by the trust; and this interest charge was non-deductible for purposes of income tax. The character and source of each item of income were determined at the level of the trust and carried through unchanged to the level of the beneficiary.

Mr. Tripet said that French law recognised the validity of a common law trust; but the tax treatment of trusts was elementary. The tax treatment was governed by five principal considerations or rules. First, following the US example, French law distinguished between revocable and irrevocable trusts; revocable trusts were ignored for tax purposes. Second, beneficiaries were taxable only on the distributed income of trusts, except that they might be taxed on the undistributed income of trusts established in tax havens. Third, as concerned the nature of income received by a beneficiary, for American trusts the rule was that the nature of the income was the same as for income received by the trust, whereas for other trusts the income in the hands of the beneficiary was treated as a dividend. However, in practice, Australian, British and Canadian trusts were assimilated to the treatment accorded to American trusts. Fourth, as concerned the residence of trusts for purposes of double tax treaties, the trust was resident in the country where it had been legally established, except that for Canadian trusts the country of residence of the trustee was the decisive consideration. A further general exception held good for trusts established in one country where the trustees' assets and/or beneficiaries were located in one or more countries. Here the location of the trust was determined by a number of different criteria in descending order of importance. Fifth, as concerned the application of double tax conventions, the beneficiary could be entitled to relief for tax withheld in the country of distribution. This relief extended only to tax withheld on the distribution to the beneficiary and not to any tax paid at the level of the trustee. The rule applied to American trusts, but was in practice extended to Australian, British and Canadian trusts.

Mr. Gillioz said that Swiss law did not recognise trusts as such. Tax practice in Switzerland on this question was fragmentary, partly because few problems had arisen in this area and few cases had been submitted to the courts. Because there were so many different kinds of trust, the tax authorities had been reluctant to speak their mind on the subject or to enunciate a firm doctrine. Trusts were ignored in Swiss law and were sometimes incompatible with the principles of Swiss law. This had been confirmed in the *Harrison case* in which Swiss authorities had sought to assimilate a foreign trust to various institutions recognised by Swiss law. A trust was different from an agency because a trust was the legal owner of trust property. However, Swiss law emphasised the economic substance of ownership rather than legal title. A trust was not a taxable entity in itself; only the beneficiaries were taxable. The details of tax liability depended on the terms of the trust. As in other countries there was a three-fold classification of trusts for this purpose. Revocable trusts were ignored for tax purposes. The income from simple trusts was taxed in the hands of the beneficiaries. For accumulation trusts the terms of the trust were decisive. Minor beneficiaries could not be taxed until they reached the age of majority. Tenants for life paid tax on the income distributed to them, but not on the capital in the trust. In general, the treatment of trusts was a grey area in Swiss law.

Dr. Killius said that German case law in this area was substantially confined to non-fiscal issues; there was very little about income tax or wealth tax. Case law needed to develop since there were few areas of certainty in the tax treatment of the beneficiary; the tax treatment of the trustee, by contrast, posed few problems since he was normally resident abroad. The principle of non-discrimination in income tax law implied that trusts should not be treated similarly to analogous institutions. There were a number of institutions resembling trusts in certain respects – family foundations, usufruct arrangements and the distinction between provisional heirs and final heirs: in each of these cases there was a distinction between the legal title to property and the economic enjoyment of the income it yielded. The establishment by a German settlor of a foreign family foundation fell between all the various stools and attracted additional liability to gift tax and income tax. In general, planning was difficult in this area. An exception was revocable trusts which were assimilated to the concept of *Treuhand* and disregarded for purposes of income tax and net worth tax. Elsewhere there was much uncertainty.

Illustrative Problems

After the coffee break, the rest of the proceedings consisted of the discussion of three problems designed to illustrate differences in approach between the countries represented on the Panel.

Problem 1

The trust was created under the laws of country A and the creator, the trustee and the trust assets were all located in country A. The sole beneficiary was resident in country B. First, if the Panelist's country was country B, would it consider the beneficiary to be taxable on all or any portion of the income derived by the trust? Second, did the answer depend on the terms of the trust? Third, if the beneficiary was taxed on the income derived through the trust, was that income characterised for tax purposes as a distribution of profits by a legal entity, or in accordance with the character of the underlying income derived by the trust, or in some other manner?

In answer to the first question, *Mr. King* said that the beneficiary, being the sole beneficiary of the trust, would be regarded as 'presently entitled' to the whole of the trust's net income at the end of the year, and would be taxable on the whole of it. In answer to the second question, he said that, provided that the beneficiary was indefeasibly entitled to the income, it did not matter that by the terms of the trust some of it would not be paid to him until a future date. The answer was therefore unaffected by the terms of the trust. A trust of this kind was regarded as a collapsible trust in Australian law. By contrast, if there was more than one beneficiary, the answer would depend on the terms of the trust. In general, distributed income was taxed in the hands of the beneficiary, and undistributed income was taxed in the hands of the trust. In answer to the third question, he said that income distributed to the beneficiary generally retained in his hands the character it had had in the hands of the trustee – for example, dividends, interest or other income.

In answer to the first question, *Mr. Tripet* said that in France the beneficiary would generally be taxable on the income; however, this answer was subject to qualifications which would be explained in the answer to question 2. In answer to the second question, he said that, if all the income was currently distributed to the beneficiary, this income would be taxable in his hands. If the trust was not established in a tax haven, the beneficiary would not be taxable until such time as the income was distributed. Beneficiaries of trusts established in tax havens, however, might be taxable even on their undistributed income. If the trust was not established in a tax haven and the trustee was given discretion to distribute or accumulate the income, the beneficiary was taxable to the extent that the income actually was distributed. In answer to the third question, he said that, if the trust was established in a tax haven, income was generally treated as the distribution of a legal entity. If the trust was established in the United States, the beneficiary's income was generally taxed in accordance with the character of the underlying income from the trust. The treatment of income from trusts established in Australia, Britain and Canada was in practice assimilated to the treatment of trusts established in the United States.

Dr. Killius said that a German administrative decree of 1968 had laid it down that the tax liability might fall either on the grantor or on the beneficiary of a trust, depending on the terms of the trust. However, this decree had not explained how the terms of the trust affected this decision; and the case law was not clear either. The question could therefore not be answered with certainty. In answer to the first question, he said that the whole income of the trust would be taxed in the hands of the beneficiary, irrespective of whether it was currently distributed or retained, if the trust were to be considered as the equivalent of a family foundation under Section 15 *Aussensteuergesetz*. In answer to the second question, he said that the tax liability of the beneficiary depended on whether the trust income was distributed to him or not. In answer to the third question he said that the income might either be treated as other periodical income or it might retain the character of the underlying income derived by the trust, depending on which theory would ultimately be adopted by the courts. There was a wide range of alternatives. However, it was doubtful whether income would retain its original character if it was left undistributed by the trust for a long period of years. There were also problems of identification when mixed income was partly distributed and partly retained.

Mr. Gillioz said that in Switzerland the answer to the first question depended on the terms of the trust: if the beneficiary was clearly designated and his designation could not be revoked, he was deemed to be the sole owner of the trust's assets and of its income. The answer to the second question was similar. If the beneficiary was clearly designated and his designation could not be revoked, he was subject to income and net worth taxes on the trust's income and assets. In answer to the third question, since the beneficiary was deemed to be the sole owner of the trust and of its income, it was the underlying income derived by the trust which was taken into account; the character of this income was not changed on distribution to him.

In answer to the first question, *Professor Dale* said that as a general rule the trust would be treated in the United States as a separate taxpayer having its own income, deductions, credits and exemptions, while the US federal income tax treatment of the beneficiary depended on the terms of the trust and various other considerations which he went on to describe. In answer to the second question, if the terms of the trust provided that the whole of its income must be distributed currently (and did not provide for the payment or setting aside of funds for charitable purposes), the amount of income that had to be distributed currently under the terms of the trust would be taxable in the hands of the beneficiary, whether or not it was actually distributed. Conversely, if the terms of the trust provided for the accumulation of trust income until some future time, the beneficiary would not be taxable until the income was distributed. However, once remitted to the beneficiary, the income of the trust would be treated as having been distributed in earlier years under the so-called 'throwback' rules. This meant that, in addition to the tax imposed on accumulation distributions to US persons from foreign trusts, a non-deductible 6% interest charge was also imposed. If the trustee had discretion either to distribute or to accumulate trust income, the beneficiary would be taxable to the extent that the trust income was in fact distributed. In answer to the third question, he said that income derived by a trust which was passed through currently to the beneficiary would generally retain the same character in the hands of the beneficiary as it had in the hands of the trust.

Problem 2

The trust was created by a resident of country A under the laws of country B. The trustee was a resident of country C where the trust assets were located. The sole beneficiary of the trust was a resident of country D. The first question was whether the Panelist's country considered the trust to be a resident for income tax purposes, if this country were respectively country A/B/C/D? Second, did the answer depend on the extent of the distribution of trust income under the terms of the trust?

In Australia the answer to the first question was yes if Australia was country C, because the trustee was then a resident of Australia. Otherwise the answer was no. A trust was only a 'resident trust estate' if either i) a trustee was a resident of Australia at any time during the relevant year of income, or ii) the central management and control of the trust was in Australia at any time during the year of income. It should be noted that the concept of a 'resident trust estate' was relevant only to the taxation of foreign income to which no beneficiary was 'presently entitled'.

In answer to the first question, France would consider the trust to be a resident for income tax purposes if France were country B, the country under the laws of which the trust had been created. Otherwise France would not consider the trust to be a resident, except that, if the trustee was a resident of Canada, then, accordance with the terms of the French-Canadian double tax treaty, France would regard the trust as resident in Canada.

Dr. Killius answered the first question for Germany country by country. Country A (country of residence of the creator of the trust). The residence of the creator of the trust could expose the trust to Geman income taxation as a resident taxpayer, if the trust was viewed as the equivalent of a family foundation or some other unincorporated entity and if the creator actually managed the investments of the trust. Nevertheless, since the creator had no power over the trust's assets or its administration, these requirements were clearly not met. Therefore, the answer was generally no. Country B (the country under the laws of which the trust was created). If the trust had been created under German law and if it were regarded as a family foundation or some other unincorporated entity, then it would have its registered seat in Germany and would therefore qualify as a German resident. Nevertheless, this question was moot, as German civil law did not permit the creation of a common law trust. Country C (the country where the trustee was resident and where the assets were located). If the trust were considered to be the equivalent of a family foundation or some other unincorporated entity, then the trustee could constitute the principal place of management of the trust. In this case the trust would be considered a German resident for German income tax purposes. Country D (the country of residence of the beneficiary). Even if the trust were regarded as the equivalent of a family foundation or some other unincorporated entity, it could not be regarded as a German resident merely because the beneficiary was a resident of Germany, in particular because the beneficiary had no power over the trust's assets or its administration. These answers were not affected by whether the trust's income was distributed or retained.

In answer to the first question, Switzerland would regard the trust as resident if Switzerland were the country of residence of the beneficiary. The considerations were similar to those already discussed under problem 1. Otherwise Switzerland would not regard the trust as resident. However, if the creator of the trust was a Swiss resident, he would be subject to gift or inheritance taxes. The residence of the trustee was irrelevant because the trustee was basically regarded as a nominee owner and in this capacity not subject to tax.

The answers to the first question for the United States were given country by country. Country A (country of residence of the creator of the trust). Although there was no meaningful statutory definition of a resident or non-resident trust for US federal income tax purposes, the United States would apparently not regard the trust as resident solely by reason of the fact that its creator was a US resident. The creator's US residence would be one factor which, in combination with other factors, would tend to cause the trust to be characterised as a US resident. Rulings and cases had established the principle that the trust's residence would depend on several factors, which would include the *situs* of the trust's creation, its place of administration and the trustee's primary residence, as well as the creator's residence. Country B (the country under whose laws the trust was established). The mere fact that the trust was formed pursuant to the laws of the United States would not be sufficient to cause the trust to be characterised as a US resident, even though it would tend to establish US residence in conjunction with additional US contacts, as indicated under country A above. Country C (country of residence of the trustee and location of the trust assets). The US residence of the trustee was a highly pertinent contact that would be accorded much weight. Standing alone it was posssible that this factor could be sufficient to establish US residence, although there was no direct authority on this point. Country D (country of residence of the beneficiary). The mere fact that the beneficiary was a US resident would not cause the trust itself to be characterised as a US resident. Many statutory provisions dealt specifically with the taxation of US beneficiaries of foreign trusts. In answer to the second question, the extent to which trust income was distributed or retained was generally of little significance in this context. In 1984 a residence test had been introduced for individuals: a 183-day rule was used in the form of a weighted average over three years. This did not apply to trusts, however, and pre-1984 precedents were therefore important in the context of the trusts. Nonetheless, results were inevitably uncertain because the weighting of the various criteria was uncertain.

Problem 3

The trust's income consisted solely of dividends from country A. The creator and the trustee were residents of country B; the trust was created under the laws of country B and wholly administered within country B. The sole beneficiary of the trust was a resident of country C. Alternative patterns of distribution were that the trust: a) distributed to the beneficiary currently an amount equal to the dividends it received from country A; b) made no current distribution to the beneficiary; and c) distributed to the beneficiary an amount equal to one half of the dividends it received from country A. There was an income tax treaty between country A and country B, reducing the country A withholding tax on dividends paid to residents of country B from 25% to 15%, but there was no income tax treaty between country A and country C. First question: if the Panelist's country was country A, the country of the source of the trust's dividend income, what rate of withholding tax was imposed under each of the three alternative distribution assumptions a), b) and c) specified above? Second question: on the alternative assumption that no tax treaty existed between country A and country B, but that the applicable treaty between country A and country C reduced the country A withholding tax on dividends paid to residents of country C from 25% to 15%, then, if the Panelist's country was country A, what rate of withholding tax was imposed under the alternative distribution assumptions a), b) and c) specified above? Third question: was the beneficiary entitled to claim a 10% refund if the 25% withholding tax was imposed by country A on the trust and the trust distributed this income to the beneficiary (a) currently, or (b) at a later date?

In Australia, the answer to the first question, case a), was in theory 25%. For the purposes of Australian domestic withholding tax laws, a beneficiary who was 'presently entitled' to a dividend included in the income of a trust estate was deemed to have derived the dividend itself. Generally, income tax treaties to which Australia was a party gave treaty benefits only to dividends beneficially derived by residents of the other country which was a party to the treaty. However, in practice, if it was not known that the payee of the dividend was a trustee, tax was imposed only at the rate of 15%. Case b). If the beneficiary was not 'presently entitled' to the dividend income which was not currently distributed to him, the withholding tax would be determined solely by reference to the status of the trustee in his capacity as the recipient of the dividends. In that case, since the trustee would not be beneficially entitled to the dividends he received, he would generally not be entitled to claim the treaty benefit of a reduced withholding tax rate. However, in practice, if it was not known that the payee of the dividend was a trustee, tax was imposed at the rate of 15%. Case c) was a mixture of cases a) and b). The answer to the second question, case a), was in theory 15%. However, in practice, if the dividend was first paid to the trustee (being the registered shareholder and a resident of country B), tax would be imposed at the rate of 25% unless and until the Australian taxation office was satisfied that the beneficiary, being a resident of country C, was 'presently entitled' to the dividend. Case b). If the beneficiary was not 'presently entitled' to the dividend income which was not currently distributed to him, then both in theory and in practice withholding tax would be levied at the rate of 25%. Case c) was a mixture of cases a) and b). Third question. Yes, the beneficiary was entitled to claim a 10% refund, whether the income was distributed to him currently or at a later date, provided that there was an income tax treaty between country A and country C and if the beneficiary could establish to the satisfaction of the Australian Taxation Office that he was 'presently entitled' to the dividend in the year of income in which it was paid to the trustee. Otherwise no.

The answer to the first question for France was that a trust was generally considered to be a resident and taxpayer of the jurisdiction under whose laws it was created. In this case, the trustee and the trust were located in country B, so that a 15% withholding tax would probably be payable, giving the trustee the benefit of the country A-country B treaty. The answer to the second question was that technically the beneficiary would not benefit from the country A-country C treaty for the reasons just stated; however, it might be possible in practice for a beneficiary to receive the reduced rate. The answer to the third question was the same.

In answer to the first question, case a), German tax treaties invaribly required the German payor of a dividend to apply a withholding tax at the regular rate of 25%, subject to a claim for refund which had to be filed by or on behalf of the recipient of the dividend. The German tax administration did not recognise a mere fiduciary (*Treuhander*) as entitled to a refund under a treaty; instead the application had to be filed by or on behalf of the grantor or beneficiary. Cases b) and c). German withholding taxes were payable when the dividend was paid out, irrespective of whether an intermediary retained the dividend or redistributed it to a beneficiary. The answer to all three cases of the second question and to both cases of the third question was that German withholding tax was imposed at the time when the dividend was received by the recipient and this applied irrespective of whether the recipient was deemed to be the trustee or the beneficiary. However, so far as the refund claim was concerned, the proper party to file such a claim would probably be the beneficiary, and it would certainly be easier to establish his standing if he could show that the trust currently distributed the German source dividends to him. Nevertheless, in the opinion of Dr. Killius, the distribution pattern should not be decisive.

For Switzerland the answers were similar to those for Germany. First question, all three cases. The rate was 25% because the beneficial owner was deemed to be the beneficiary and not the trustee. Second question, all three cases. The rate was 15% because the beneficiary was considered to be the beneficial owner. In answer to the third question, the beneficiary was in both cases entitled to claim a refund within the time limits specified by the tax treaty.

The answer to the first question, case a), for the United States was that the gross income of a trust was computed in the same way as the gross income of an individual; a foreign trust, as a non-resident entity, would be taxed generally in the same manner as the non-resident alien individual. Accordingly, the US source dividend paid to the trust would, in the first instance, be subject to a 15% withholding tax, regardless of the residence status of the beneficiary. However, the beneficiary would be required to include in his income the amounts distributed to him by the trust and such income would be considered to have the same source and character as it had in the hands of the trust. Accordingly, the beneficiary would be subject to the 25% (withholding) tax rate, and the 15% tax withheld initially on the payment to the trust would be deemed to have been paid by the beneficiary. The trust would therefore be required to withhold the additional 10% tax when remitting the income to the beneficiary, notwithstanding its status as a non-resident for US income tax purposes. If the trust failed to withhold, the beneficiary would be required to file a US tax return and pay such tax. Case b). The same general principles would hold good in case b) (no current distribution) except that the throwback rules would also apply. Case c) was a mixture of a) and b). The answer to question 2, case a), was that the 25% rate of withholding tax would apply initially on the payment of the dividend to the trust, and the beneficiary would be required to claim a refund for the excess withholding tax of 10%. Case b). Once again, the 25% tax which could continue to be withheld initially on the payment to the trust would be deemed to have been paid by the beneficiary and the excess withholding tax would have to be recovered through a refund claim. The third question was covered by the answers to questions 1 and 2. In general, the principle governing US tax law in this area was that each step stood on its own and had to be considered separately.

As there was no time to discuss the remaining problems, Professor Dale thanked the Panelists and declared the Seminar closed.

III. APPENDIX: PROBLEMS

Problem 1

'Trust' is created under the laws of 'Country A' by 'Creator', a resident of Country A. The 'Trustee' of the trust, also a resident of Country A, holds and administers the assets of the trust Country A. The sole beneficiary of the trust, 'Beneficiary', is a resident of Country B. Neither Creator nor beneficiary has any power over the trust's assets or it's administration. All of the trust's income is derived from investments in Country A.

1. If your country were Country B, would it consider beneficiary to be taxable on all or any portion of the income derived by trust?

2. Does the answer depend upon whether by the terms of the trust:

(i) all of the income is distributed currently to beneficiary?

(ii) all of the income is accumulated until some future time?

(iii) the income may be distributed or accumulated in the discretion of the trustee?

3. If beneficiary is taxed on income derived through the trust, is that income characterized for tax purposes as a distribution of profits by a legal entity, in accordance with the character of the underlying income derived by trust, or in some other manner?

Problem 2

'Trust' is created under the laws of 'Country B' by 'Creator', a resident of 'Country A'. The 'Trustee' of the trust is a resident of 'Country C' and holds and administers the assets of the trust in Country C. The sole beneficiary of the trust, 'Beneficiary', is a resident of 'Country D'. Neither Creator nor beneficiary has any power over the trust's assets or its administration.

1. Would your country consider the trust to be a resident for income tax purposes if:

(a) if it were Country A?

(b) if it were Country B?

(c) if it were Country C?

(d) if it were Country D?

2. Does the answer depend upon whether by the terms of the trust:

(i) all of the income is distributed currently to beneficiary?

(ii) all of the income is accumulated until some future time?

(iii) the income may be distributed or accumulated in the discretion of the trustee?

Problem 3

'Trust' is created under the laws of 'Country B' by 'Creator', who is a resident of Country B, and is administered by 'Trustee', also a resident of Country B, wholly within Country B. 'Beneficiary' is the sole beneficiary of the trust and is a resident of 'Country C'. Neither Creator nor beneficiary has any power over the trust's assets or its administration. Trust's only income consists of dividends derived from 'Country A'. Assume alternatively that the trust: (a) distributes to beneficiary currently an amount equal to the dividends; (b) makes no current distribution to beneficiary; and (c) distributes to beneficiary an amount equal to one-half of the dividends. Assume further that the applicable income tax treaty between Country A and Country B reduces the Country A withholding tax on dividends paid to residents of Country B from 25% to 15% but that there is no income tax treaty between Country A and Country C.

1. If your country is Country A, what rate of withholding tax is imposed under each of the three alternative distribution assumptions specified above:

(a) current distribution to beneficiary?
(b) no current distribution?
(c) partial distribution?

2. Assume, instead, that no tax treaty exists between Country A and Country B but that the applicable treaty between Country A and Country C reduces the Country A withholding tax on dividends paid to residents of Country C from 25% to 15%; if your country is Country A, what rate of withholding tax is imposed under the alternative distribution patterns:

(a) current distribution to beneficiary?
(b) no current distribution?
(c) partial distribution?

3. May beneficiary claim a 10% refund if the 25% withholding tax is imposed by Country A upon the trust and the trust distributes such income to beneficiary:

(a) currently?
(b) at a later date?

Problem 4

'Trust' is created under the laws of 'Country B' by 'Creator', who is a resident of Country B, and is administered by 'Trustee', also a resident of Country B, wholly within Country B. 'Beneficiary' is the sole beneficiary of the trust and is a resident of 'Country C'. Neither Creator nor beneficiary has any power over the trust's assets or its administration. Trust's only income consists of dividends derived from 'Country A'. Assume alternatively that trust: (a) distributes to beneficiary currently an amount equal to the dividends; (b) makes no current distribution to beneficiary; and (c) distributes to beneficiary an amount equal to one-half of the dividends. Your country is Country C, in which beneficiary is resident.

1. If a Country A withholding tax is paid by the trust upon its receipt of the dividend income, is beneficiary entitled to claim a foreign tax credit under Country C law for this amount when he takes the income into account?

2. If relevant (as in computing a per-country foreign tax credit limitation), is the income deemed to have its source in Country A or in Country B?

3. If Country B imposes a tax on the dividend income when received by the trust (allowing a foreign tax credit for the Country A tax), can the beneficiary claim any relief by way of credit or offset against his Country C tax for the tax imposed by Country B when the income remaining after this tax is distributed?

Problem 5

1. Assume that in each of the cases described above Problems 1 through 4 that the 'Creator' of 'Trust', has the power to revoke the trust and repossess its assets. What is the effect of such a power on the answers to each of the questions asked above?

2. In the alternative, what is the effect if the 'Beneficiary', rather than the 'Creator', has the power to require the trust assets to be transferred to him in whole or part?

www.ingramcontent.com/pod-product-compliance
Lightning Source LLC
Chambersburg PA
CBHW071359230926
51846CB00002B/594
* 9 7 8 9 0 6 5 4 4 3 4 6 5 *